Pombreol

My Hero

Pombreol

My Hero

by

Stella Sondpi

Nenge Books

Pombreol - My Hero
by Stella Sondpi

copyright © Stella Sondpi 2021

All rights reserved.

This book or parts thereof may not be reproduced in any form, stored in a mechanical retrieval system or transmitted in any form by any means - electronic, mechanical, photocopy, recording or otherwise - without prior written permission of the publisher.

Design, desktop and editing by Nenge Books
Published by Nenge Books, Australia, 2021
ABN 26809396184
nengebooks1@gmail.com
www.nengebooks.com

Nenge Books publishes quality books using cost effective print-on-demand technology to enable independent authors to publish. Enquiries from authors are welcome.

ISBN 978-0-6488206-7-3

Dedication

To my three precious young jewels (Zebedee, Shadrach and Sorwa Joy), I hope you can embrace the rich culture and heritage that are found in this story.

CONTENTS

INTRODUCTION	ix
WAR LORDS, BLOODSHED & TITLES	1
COURTSHIP	8
DIVISON OF LABOUR	18
TRADE	25
SINGSING & PIG KILL	37
RITUAL INITIATION INTO ADULTHOOD	53
DEATH, CAUSES & AFTERLIFE	58
CEREMONIAL EXCHANGE	66
BETRAYAL OF CLANSMEN & CONSEQUENCES	80
MARRIAGE	85
SACRIFICES TO THE SPIRITS	95
MOONLIGHT HUNTING	109
THE SPIRITS MUST BE ANGRY AGAIN	115
DREAMS ARE NOT JUST DREAMS	128
INTO THE HANDS OF THE ENEMY	132
STRANGE HAPPENINGS	140
HUMANS OR GODS???	145
THE OLD HAS GONE & THE NEW HAS COME	159
About the Author	169

INTRODUCTION

History records that Portuguese and Spanish Navigators sailing in the early 16th century were the first Europeans to locate the island of New Guinea. In time Australia became the colonial administrator of Papua and New Guinea but their influence was limited to the coastal areas only. During those colonial days nobody thought people were actually living beyond the mountains, therefore there was no real attempt to explore and map out the mountainous interior.

The chain of mountains was difficult to traverse so it was presumed that nobody could possibly be living there. Yet in those rugged interiors, there were people living completely disconnected from the rest of the world. People who had their own styles and ways of living. People who had been completely isolated from the outside world as their own travels were limited and it was far too dangerous to travel outside the safety of their own territory. People who had successfully learnt to earn their living by the mercy of Mother Nature, who provided for them from the series of fertile valleys in between the mountains.

They lived in tribal groups having their own network of enemies, allies, trade systems, barter systems, health care system, worship system, and so on. It was absolutely a lost world of people completely isolated from rest of the world. This group of people were basically living a Stone Age existence.

However, in 1930, gold prospecting Australians Michael, Daniel and James Leahy, known commonly as the Leahy Brothers, led an expedition into the Highlands of New Guinea and discovered that people were actually living beyond the mountains. This was contradictory to the original belief based on presumption. In the Wahgi Valley in the Western Highlands Province the Leahy brothers built an airstrip, after inspection by air. This was meant to be the first airstrip in this part of the world and was going to be the main entry of civilisation to the rest of the Highlands Region.

Beyond them to the west lay yet another group of high mountains that surrounded the Mt.Hagen area, and another population of people that the Leahy Brothers knew nothing about. They were the Mendi Valley People from what is now known as Southern Highlands Province. This group of people had their first contact with the outside world only in 1950 when Methodist and Catholic Missionaries and Government Patrol Officers from the coastal areas walked into their land.

This book therefore captures all the drama of the historic encounter that would change the lives of these unsuspecting, innocent people for a lifetime. The book is written so readers can understand what life was like in the Stone Age lifestyles of this group of people before the relatively recent arrival of the white man.

I believe that the rich cultural heritage being discussed in this book is fast disappearing as young people of our land no longer take heed of the importance of our rich cultures and way of Life. It is my heart's desire that our people do not forget their identity. That our cultures, customs and traditions are highly valued as they represent our people's unique contribution to the country and the world - it is our identification.

God made us special with all these unique cultures and traditions, handed down to us by our forefathers who had just been introduced to the outside world in the early 1950s. Our children should not be encouraged to think that our cultures, traditions and our way of living belongs to our ancestors, therefore are dirty and primitive. After all, which cultures in the whole wide world were not primitive before technology arrived?

Most of us are who we are because our way of life helped develop, mould and shape our attitudes and characteristics to be productive in our own societies and the wider world. We are who we are as we come out of a society and culture that is ours alone. A culture that is rich, colourful, unique and has its roots deep down in our own society.

When we are living by other people's cultures, we are living a borrowed life. When we borrow something, it's not ours; therefore we have no roots and it will only confuse our future generations. The blending of our cultures with Western culture is killing our cultures and we face a huge challenge on how to preserve and record our rich heritage in this country.

In fact, not everything done by our forefathers was right and needs preservation. For instance, the brutal killing of the enemies or the practices of witchcraft and sorcery described in this book. In such evil practices, the Gospel's light and God's Grace had been at work in the cultures preparing the hearts of people to receive the gospel and the true light that only the gospel can bring. Thankfully, we can now see the gospel of truth also working within our cultures.

However, we must never forget that there were other unique practices that have been preserved so our children know and have an identity rooted in our unique culture. These are at risk of being lost with Western influences if not preserved and passed on to future generations.

Because I wanted to make a contribution to preserving this important aspect of our origins, I have tried my best to describe in detail our cultures and traditions, presented in a story form so as to attract young people's attention, for most people in this part of the world like reading stories. Not only will they enjoy reading the stories but will also learn the traditions and culture practiced by our forefathers, which are fast disappearing.

There have been documentaries done in Australia on the first contact. They were done from the point of view of the New Arrivals. The local people's views were taken from the Waghi Valley people of the Western Highlands Province. However, this book is written in detail from the viewpoint of the Stone Age people of the Mendi Valley in the Southern Highlands Province. It discusses what really took place in that Stone Age lifestyle of the children of the Mendi valley, and the reaction to the arrival of outside influence.

It discusses tribal fights, bloodshed, warlords, courtship, marriage, bride price, traditional healing, beliefs, gods, worship, leadership, delegations of jobs, tools, wealth, trade and barter systems. It finally narrates the arrival of the white man - from the perspective of the native people.

I am an acute care nurse working as a Nurse Administrator at Mendi Hospital. The book is written from stories handed down to me by my grandad who is the main character in the stories. I am forever grateful for this invaluable information and knowledge he had left with me before he departed this world in the year 2000.

I hope my three precious young jewels (Zebedee, Shadrach and SorwaJoy) embrace the rich culture and heritage that is discussed in this book.

Pombreol, the main character in this book, was my maternal grandfather and I was privileged to have been brought up by him. He related all these stories to me. I remember him as a loving yet fearful grandad who will always be my Hero.

Sr.Stella Sondpi
March 2021
Mendi, SHP

One

WAR LORDS, BLOODSHED & TITLES

By the side of the silently flowing creek everything had suddenly grown quieter and colder. Even the night animals were still as they began to sense something extraordinary was about to happen. Perhaps they were sensing the inner conflict of the young man lying stiff, curled up and shivering uncontrollably under the dense forest canopy. Soon the attack on their most hated enemy would begin. The endless darkness was fading as the morning sun began brightening up the day from the east.

Pombreol was cold and rigid. He'd had to lie still in the freezing darkness for quite a long time, waiting for the right hour of attack. While rubbing his stiff fingers together to get some warmth into his almost frozen body, he wondered why they couldn't simply attack these people in their sleep rather than waiting through the cold, never-ending night.

Pombreol

They had been his tribe's bitter enemies for as long as he could remember. He had asked his old man several times about that, but his father on every occasion would always give the same answer.

"It's unmanly to kill people in their sleep, only cowards who don't know how to fight would do that." And he would always conclude, "Son, to become a real warrior you've got to give your enemy the chance to defend themselves instead of murdering them in their sleep."

He slowly got up with those words ringing in his ears as if they were just spoken yesterday, knowing full well that this was his first time to lead an attack in a tribal fight - though he had fought under other leaders and killed several men already. Anyway, he couldn't go back now. He had to become a great warrior. This was the custom for whoever led an ambush and came home victorious. They gained a fearfully recognised position in the clan.

Earlier Pombreol had sworn to himself that he would fight to his last breath if this could make his dying old man proud and bring a smile to his forever gloomy and depressing face. Worried that no one was taking his place as one of the greatest warriors who ever lived, the old man thought all his sons were becoming cowards. If someone was going to illuminate his face, it had to be young Pombreol, and this was the chance, as whispers were that the old man was to go and be with the dead ancestors any moment soon.

The jungle surroundings were now wide awake with tiny movements. The rest of the tribesmen silently got their bows and arrows ready as they waited for the whistle from Pombreol, the leader of today's attack.

They had come a long way for this attack, and now the time had come for the upcoming warrior to give orders. Some had their own doubts about him, but as he stood there giving orders, which man was to go where and with whom, he looked fearsome enough.

As they moved forward, being very careful not to make any noise, they heard the strike of a bow from the opposing tribesmen. Pombreol and his men knew their enemies were on the lookout and were now attacking the men who had been sent to the rear. More strikes and arrows came flying at them. As Pombreol and his men struck back in retaliation there were cries of pain from both sides.

The sun was now high in the sky, there was fierce fighting going on. Men were falling back and the enemies were advancing on Pombreol's men. It seemed all his men were overpowered.

Pombreol hadn't received any wound yet though he was close to receiving some. By now he sensed that enemies were surrounding him. He also knew they wanted him alive so that they could torture him before killing him. He had killed several of that tribe's men since the tribal warfare started a few months ago.

The fight was over one piece of land that the enemy was wrongly claiming. It belonged to his tribesmen. Ever since he was a small boy this particular tribal enemy clan had always instigated problems, and he was pissed off this time. He will make sure they feel the pain of his arrow.

Common sense however told him to run away, but he could not now. He had to look for his smaller brother, as was the custom. Brothers who want to fight together must bring the other home dead or alive unless all have been killed because the spirit has no resting place in an enemy's land. It is difficult to call for a dead spirit in enemy territory too.

Where was his brother now? They were supposed to be fighting back to back, but his brother was nowhere to be seen. The enemies were dangerously close to closing in on him and he was getting desperate now.

Oh, Songo, what was the colour of the paint he was painted with? Was it red and black or pure black? Black and white! Oh, yes, he remembered now. He had to be here somewhere! Pombreol had to look more carefully to find his brother or he would be called a coward for the rest of his life, and all his relentless planning for this attack on the enemy would be a terrible waste.

He would rather die than be called a coward by the people whose approval he was seeking. It was now or never. With an urgency that was growing strong from within him, he looked around in pure desperation. To his great joy, he saw his brother lying on the ground with an arrow stuck through both of his lower legs.

He lowered himself to the ground and crawled towards his brother. The crawl was long and hard, despite the fact that the distance was very short. At any moment, arrows could come flying towards him and the shot could be fatal. Therefore he crawled carefully towards his wounded brother who was now staring at him with a renewed hope.

Before he knew about his brother's very risky and life threatening rescue mission, Songo was just staring into the space knowing this was the end of his life as he had no other choice with both of his legs wounded.

Songo could not believe that his elder brother came back for him and tried to roll himself towards him, but

Pombreol was beside him already. Upon reaching his brother, Pombreol whispered to him to roll himself onto his shoulder and hold on tightly.

With strength he never knew he possessed, he lifted his brother up onto his shoulders and tried to run back to where his clansmen were. Knowing full well that his enemies were advancing on the two of them, he had to get out of there as fast as possible.

His brother hung onto him and squeezed him so tight that he felt his very breath was almost squeezed out of him.

"I have to shoot at enemies now so, lest you fall, hold onto me tightly," he told his brother.

Noticing that the attack was getting weaker, the enemy had advanced on Pombreol and his tribesmen rapidly from almost all directions. Pombreol desperately shot at the advancing enemies faster and faster until all his arrows were gone. Unfortunately he had now used up all his arrows, and without those precious arrows, he felt helpless and trapped. In pure desperation he looked around but could not find any more weapons to fight his enemies.

To his great relief his brother still had his arrows with him. Using those, he killed several men who were pursuing him. Meanwhile his clansmen, after realising that Pombreol and his brother were miraculously still alive, came back for their rescue and joined them in the fight. The enemies then retreated.

Pombreol's tribe lost three men. Seven others were injured that day. It was a fight never to be forgotten. However, they were coming home victorious, and for now, that was all Pombreol wanted.

Meanwhile the old men, women and children in the village had prepared a big feast for their men, as well as for themselves. They had been fasting from the minute the men left for the battle field.

It had always been the practice for those remaining behind to go without food while their men were at war. If someone did eat, it was a sure thing that their family member out in battle field would be killed. Therefore even the children waited patiently for the return of Pombreol and his men. Everybody was anxious.

Silence fell all over the village as the sad sound of the bamboo flute was heard at the lookout point. The music told them there were some deaths. With tears everyone ran to meet them.

They knew they couldn't cry out loud, because their enemies would think they had won the battle and start celebrating with loud provocative songs. They couldn't afford to give them that opportunity, for their pride would be wounded.

Pombreol was leading with his brother over his shoulder and a wounded cousin supported by his arm. To the people who went forward to greet them, he truly looked like a hero.

His two wives, who had married him at the same time, were among the group. They stood around and were shy despite the fact that they were overjoyed to see that he was not only safe but also a hero. Obvious displays of emotions were unheard of. This was his day, a day that all the family had been waiting for.

The happiest of all was Pombreol's old father. As he stood watching his son arriving this way, he felt something wet on his cheeks. He couldn't believe it; he was actually crying.... a proud old man.... Why should he be ashamed of crying? These were tears of joy, because his dream had come true at last. One of his own flesh and blood had led a tribal fight and had come home victorious.

His son was a real warrior returning from battle, with head held high and also carrying his wounded brother. He was sure someone had taken over his place, so he was ready to go and be with his ancestors.

Pombreol looked at his two wives and the two young babies who were busily sucking at their mothers' bare breasts. Then he stole a glance at his father, who gave a smile of approval that lit up his whole wrinkled and gloomy face.

Pombreol felt a joy like he had never felt before, for he truly knew that he had made his father proud. Though he almost got killed, it was a fight that was worth it as he had won the the title of great warrior.

Two

COURTSHIP

After that attack, Pombreol was declared a great warrior. The number in his household increased, and he became a man of wealth and a great leader.

He took a third wife and she fell pregnant. His other two wives and their two children each slept in the women's and children's long house.

It had three different fireplaces and three doors all facing the direction of the sunrise. He built them this way so that his wives and children would feel the morning warmth of the sun.

The tribesmen's dwelling house was hot and smoky. One night, Pombreol needed some fresh air and wanted to be in the bright moonlight. This was a good night to go hunting but he couldn't for he knew the bright moonlight would disappear shortly. It was just the first day of the moonlit night and therefore this bright light that had quickly lit up the whole earth would disappear just as fast as it had come. Maybe he could go hunting the day after tomorrow. Usually on the third day, the light would last for hours.

He stood there in the moonlight feeling cold in the highlands night. In his wives' house he heard the pigs making hungry noises and the ladies feeding them with kaukau. In the midst of all that he heard one of his children crying and the mother smacking him repeatedly. As he listened to his son weeping, he felt like going into the ladies' house and beating the hell out of those women, but he controlled himself. He was a warrior so he could not break tradition by being found in a woman's house. Knowing that tomorrow his temper would cool down, he walked aimlessly up and down wondering how in the world he had ended up with this woman who was never submissive.

Now his mind went off to the first time he had seen this woman, now his second wife, at a courting party.

The boys from his tribe had gone to court the girls of the next clan one moonlit night like tonight. During the day the boys sent a message through another young girl that they were coming. All the young girls gathered in the courting house to prepare for their arrival.

As he entered the courting house he tripped over something and fell down on top of someone sitting in the dark next to the doorway. Without much thought, he got up quickly, apologized to whoever it was and sat down where the boys were sitting.

The young girls sat on their side, lined up, and sang their courting songs. The boys on the other side of the fireplace answered with boys' courting songs. The words of the songs contained names of lovely rivers, beautiful lands and cool mountains that were distinctive in his village.

This went on for a while until the girls sang their final song inviting the boys to go sit next to their girlfriends or the girls they wanted to court. The one married woman who was asked to keep the fire going all through the night did her job, which was to supervise the whole courting event. So she had to stay awake through the whole night. If she fell asleep, disaster might happen among all the young people and she would carry all the blame.

Pombreol didn't need to wait for the invitation to be given out by the womenfolk with their special invitation songs, because his engaged girlfriend was among them. Getting up quickly, he was the first one to go and sit beside her. It was always like that with her. There was always something that pulled him to her and his heart always beat faster when he was near her.

The bravest guy makes the first move. In other courting parties he could sit around and let others make the first move but with this group of girls, he was always the first one; there was always a unseen force that pulled him towards her.

As he studied her with a few quick glances, she sat in a stiff and elegant way, gathering her grass skirt in between her folded legs, and a piece of apron from string made from traditional ropes firmly placed around her breasts.

As he sat close to her, he observed that she did not seem to be frightened or even affected by his closeness to her in the dark, unlike some other girls he knew. He knew in his heart that she had also accepted him. The very thought of it made him shiver despite the heat of the crowded house.

His cousin's girlfriend was the next in line so Tombe was the next one beside her with several other boys all sitting beside their girl. Those two girls have always sat beside each other and have been everywhere together since they were the girlfriends of the two blood related cousins.

The remaining boys and girls continued their songs while the boys with their girlfriends started a special tune of songs called the *'tumen'*.

The *tumen* was not just a courtship song but it told about the beauty of places, people and lifestyles. The words of the song would make the climbing of the highest mountain like ascending a small hill, the driest land absolutely fertile, and even the ugliest person in the team the most beautiful.

A dead heart would awaken as it beat so fast and strong against one's rib bones. Emotions ran high as each individual man lamented with his special song (*tumen*) for every women sitting beside him.

The rhythm of it would sound like the song was only meant for each other. As the rhythm softly rose and fell in the still of the dark, nothing else mattered except each other.

As for Pombreol, he felt he was flying so high and floating on some light clouds. He knew he would land anytime, but not just now. Not as long as he was beside this woman. He felt like he could spend eternity beside her.

Right now, if he had completely exhausted himself of all the *tumen* songs that his father taught him, it wouldn't matter, for he would compose his own songs. He was sure she wouldn't mind. The reponse she gave him as soon as he completed one song was just right. She truly was the best thing that had ever happened to him.

He could feel their hearts beating loudly together and they even seemed to be breathing at the same time!

Pombreol had to touch himself to make sure this was real - they were two different people just connected for tonight only.

Somehow, the supervisor must have sensed it too as she put more dry sticks into the slowly glowing flame and extra light was produced. Pombreol came back to his normal self again.

Soon the courting songs progressed into full swing as emotions ran high, ordinary movements were made extraordinary and good things even better with the words of the courting songs.

Pombreol was really enjoying himself as he sat beside this woman he dearly held close to his heart day and night. Everytime he sat close to this woman his hormones would create havoc in his whole system. Everything would just get tangled within him. All of a sudden, his heart would beat very fast and whole body would become so weak as if he had no control over his very own body.

It did not take very long for him to realize he had fallen for her more than any other woman in the whole wide world. If for some reason she didn't marry him, he might as well die as he could never ever imagine another day without her. He thought he would just be half of himself without her and so he needed her to become a complete man.

Sometimes he wondered if she really loved him and it would drive him crazy the moment he thought about it.

As he was starting his seventh *tumen* he heard men shouting outside. Nobody paid any attention because the courting was at its highest peak and there was lots of noise inside the courting house. One more shout outside and pieces of flattened wood fell upon each

Pombreol

other as a door at the entrance collapsed and curtains of dry banana leaves flew in all directions. Suddenly all noise inside stopped. Even the active lady supervisor was speechless. All had gone suddenly silent.

In the quiet of the dark night one man outside asked if Pombreol was inside. If he was inside, he might as well come out now so all are not disturbed.

Goodness, what was going on? This was no enemy tribe. Had these clansmen given permission to the enemy to come and kill Pombreol and his boys on their land? While all this was going on in his mind, the noise outside got louder and more abusive.

"Pombreol, you come out and explain to us why you touched the breast and body of our girl." Pombreol couldn't believe that he was being accused of a serious crime he had never committed.

He hoped that he was having a bad dream from which he would wake anytime. When he found his voice he told them he did no such things.

"Is that how you deny your actions? From others you might escape, but not from us." The owner of the voice was a tough looking middle aged man. His six sons all looked serious and the daughter was with him.

Pombreol couldn't remember seeing or courting a girl like this, therefore he further denied it. He struggled in the dark to play around with his memory to recall this girl, but this time his usually very active memory failed him. He couldn't remember seeing this girl let alone holding her breast, as those fierce looking brothers declared.

When the girl was made to talk at last, she said it was in this very courting house that he had intentionally fallen on top of her and touched her breast and other parts of her body that she really wasn't about to go into details about.

As she was talking Pombreol could feel his beloved one sitting next to him going stiff. A shiver ran down his spine for he had seen girls leave their fiancés because they were betrayed.

But he hadn't done anything and he couldn't afford to lose her. Therefore breaking all laws, he reached over in the dark, grabbed her hand and pulled her towards him. Desperately, he whispered that she had to believe that he hadn't done anything to betray her and she was the only woman in his life, there surely was no other.

He squeezed her hand so tightly and held onto it as if his very life depended on it. He released her hand only when she reassured him with a positive nod of her head to let him know that she trusted him.

Pombreol tried to explain his part of the story but the girl's relatives wouldn't have it.

"You have made our girl useless and when other young boys hear of this, they won't pay the bride price. You will have to take her as your wife," they demanded.

Pombreol was angry with them but he had no choice so he took her with him. His engaged girlfriend came away with him on the same day, too, because she refused to give her boyfriend over to her own clan's women. He was so happy she made that decision that all unhappiness of the night vanished.

His father paid bride price for both women at the same time, making both of them his wives. But Pombreol always treated the woman who he wanted to be his wife as the first. Seeing that, the other one always had a rebellious attitude, and that bothered him. Now they both had two children each. Surely, he had seen to that.

The moon suddenly disappeared behind the black cloud and he was feeling cold now. In the distance he heard a night bird singing. The noises in the women's house settled. The pigs had been fed and were sleeping.

The crying boy had gone to his third wife and she was telling him the legend about the old man and old woman who went searching for food in an old abandoned garden. It went like this:

"An old man was standing on a traditional ladder post cutting down bananas from a banana tree. When he was coming down he slipped off and unfortunately injured one of his testicles. Taking it out, he gave it to his old woman, requesting her to take special care of his precious cargo. Back at home, the old man asked for his testicle but she couldn't locate it. He was so angry he got a big stick and hit her and she fought back. They fought until morning and then went their separate ways. The man went upstream and she went downstream of the Wara Lai."

Pombreol heard the boy go off to sleep and remembered how, as a small boy, he begged his mother over and over again to tell that same story again and again. He never got tired of listening to this short legend and he was sure his mum never grew weary of telling him those short stories.

He would do extra errands for her just to hear them. The legends became extra-ordinary when she changed the tone of her voice and chanted the words away in extra-ordinary tunes. It was a special melody to his sleepy ears. Oh, how he missed his own mum now.

He felt sad now that his mother, who always seemed strong, had gone forever. He never once imagined his mum would depart from his life forever.

Anyway, he must get some rest so he could get up early for the taro planting the next day. He walked quietly back to the men's hut and found that it was pitch dark inside the house. The fire light had reduced its glow. With sleep gone, he lay curled up on his side contentedly listening to the familiar sounds around him; the regular breathing and occasional snores of the men and young boys were comforting sounds at times like this.

Pombreol lay on the hard earth floor listening to all this noise, forgetting the grunts and snuffles of the pigs from his recent trip to the ladies' house. His back was pressed comfortably against one of the men who were snoring softly next to him.

It was not cold as the fire has been kept burning low by one of the men in the house who had wakened and walked about in the night. With the comfort of the warmth of the fire and the others sleeping beside him, he fell into a deep sleep, listening to the wind making soft, rustling murmurs in the grassy roof. He had fallen into a sweet but deep, deep sleep.

Then he heard a sound which had him instantly fully awake. It was the croak, croak, croak of the frogs as they set about their business of waking the people and announcing the approaching day light. As the frogs ceased their croaking, Pombreol knew that soon the first glimmers of daybreak would be lighting up the eastern sky.

Slowly so as not to wake up the other sleepers alongside him, he crawled out of his snug position and stood up, slowly stretching himself, and stole quietly toward the door, bending down only to open the door. Heavy pieces of wood which were thrust into slots on either side of the door and placed upon each other were pulled out, and he bent down and crawled outside.

He was sure he was the only person awake on this clear and cool morning. He breathed in the crisp fresh air deeply while blowing out of his lungs the stuffiness of the smoke laden air from a night inside a windowless house.

The wind had swept the sky clear of the clouds and the big, glistening morning star hung motionless in the east, gradually growing paler as the sun's faint first beams spread across the horizon, enlightening the sleeping valley.

He watched with eager eyes as the sun, a blinding ball of brightness, rose over the hills throwing large slabs of golden lights everywhere.

Soon the top of the hill that towered on the other side of the mighty Lai River was covered with sunshine and he knew it was time to gear up his family for the taro planting. The family had a hard day ahead so each member had to be awake.

Three

DIVISON OF LABOUR

By now everyone was awake and his son by the first wife brought Pombreol breakfast of sweet potato from the third and first wives.

The second wife hadn't sent anything and he knew why. She was the one making a fire very early in the small house that accommodates women having their monthly cycle. That wasn't good because she wouldn't come to the garden to plant the taro garden.

"Nawe, go tell your mother to look after all the pigs while we are out in the garden planting."

"But father, there is lots of planting to be done and why can't she come and help?"

Knowing that the boy would continue asking until he got the answer, Pombreol told him, "If she comes to help plant the taro, it won't grow properly and those that have grown will be eaten by ground beetles, causing a poor harvest. Son, you must understand too that taro is a men's crop and we have to repay those taros that were given to us in the last harvest. Therefore we can't allow improper plantings."

Pombreol

Nawe still looked confused. "But father I still don't understand why harvest will be very poor if my second mother helps."

If this was someone else asking questions he would not answer at all since the boy was disturbing his breakfast. But this was his favourite son by his favourite wife, so he patiently answered. "She is unclean now that she is staying in that ladies' small house. Such ladies can't come near our taro garden, let alone go inside. Now go get ready and no more questions, and remember not to go near that small house or even accept food from such ladies or you won't grow well." In fact Nawe had lots to ask but he heard that final note in his father's voice and ran off to get ready.

Pombreol knew soon the sun would rise with its fierce heat and work would be almost impossible in the garden. So he started off to the garden with his bow and arrow alert, watching for danger from wild animals or enemies. Should there be an attack of any kind, he was always ready to defend his family.

The women struggled behind with heavy loads of taro seeds and other necessary seedlings for the planting. The other wife was more burdened by the bundle of a sleeping baby on top of the seedling bag. Her piglet followed her from behind.

It had taken Pombreol quite a time to clear this land. He'd felled trees and cut them up with his sharp stone axe. He had cleared away trees, bush and grass before the women started to come into the garden to plough the land. With the help of his sons he'd also built a very strong fence around the garden to keep wild pigs from destroying his gardens.

Pombreol

He almost lost his precious stone axe in the drain left by his forefathers when they planted the garden in their times. He was struggling to chop down a huge tree when the stone axe slide off the handle and fell into the ditch.

He searched and searched in the mud until he found his precious stone axe, vowing never to be careless again. If he lost this one, he wouldn't know where to get another one quickly. It had cost his grandfather a great deal of wealth to get this one that had been passed down to him from his father.

This piece of land had always produced the best taros and he was sure this harvest would not be an exception. Pombreol remembered the great harvest his own parents had on this very land when he was a young boy. He was almost the size of his own son who was now working so hard silently at his side.

By the time they reached the garden the sun had climbed high above Mount Giluwe and was bathing the beautiful green valley and grassy slopes in its warmth and brightness. It was time to work.

Out in the garden the sun was very hot but Pombreol drove his family hard the whole day. Each member of the family carried out their responsibilities in total silence. He did all the hole digging in rows while Nawe and Heranong, the first daughter of the second wife, passed the taro plants to the two ladies to plant.

As the sun climbed higher in the bright blue sky its hot beams beat down on the family labouring in the garden, but there was work to be done and they kept on silently, listening only to each other's deep breaths.

The main portion of the garden was for taro but there was a small portion of ground for sweet potatoes, which was their day to day food. The ash from the burnt rubbish was reserved for special foods like cucumbers, a type of asparagus and several varieties of greens. Corn and beans were also planted between the taros.

Pombreol knew the family was exhausted from the day's work but he wanted each member of the family to complete their delegated duties, so he kept working. He was sure to have enough to feed his family and repay people for the taro he had received during their harvest. People would then know that he was not only good at tribal fights but also a strong man capable of planting taro like a real man, and repaying his debts. He also planned to cook some during the big feast called the 'saida' or the great feast which was to take place after twelve full moons.

They worked until late evening when the taro seeds were all planted. The family gathered their working tools and walked slowly home in pure exhaustion - and unbearable hunger. As they neared home they could hear activities going on in the house. The young daughter who was tasked to look after the pigs was feeding them. This was evident by the pig's hungry screams, which they could hear from a distance as they slowly approached their dwelling place.

Pombreol's mind was not on feeding pigs but feeding his stomach. He felt so hungry he could eat anything at this time. He believed his whole family was feeling the same thing. A decent meal was the first thing on his mind.

Pombreol and his son Nawe waited outside the house while the ladies went in to find their young daughter. Thankfully she had already prepared enough sweet potatoes for the whole family, cooked in the hot ashes produced by the open fire in the house. She removed them out of the cooking place and got them all ready for the family, who shared among themselves and ate hungrily.

Pombreol and the elder son were also given their share of the meal. Because they were male they got the biggest and best share. They started eating as soon as the food reached them as they walked to the men's dwelling place. Without joining the conversation, father and son walked straight to their sleeping place and fell asleep immediately. They were too exhausted to keep their eyes open even for another minute. The day's work has been too much.

Early the next day, Pombreol's wives and daughters went back to the new garden to complete the planting. Each woman was given their own piece of land to work on, so they worked the whole day again to plant the other seeds like the corn, cabbage and bean seeds.

By midday, a few dark clouds were seen gathering in the sky and a very cold wind began blowing towards the north. A few drops of rain started falling on one of the lady's bare brown back and made her call out, "We had better get going or soon we will get wet". However, Pombreol's wives decided that the rain was light and kept on working in the garden.

The planting of the whole garden was completed by the end of the day. Everybody was exhausted but all were in good spirits as their garden was complete and they were all looking forward to their harvest.

As they gathered their personal belongings to head home they saw that thick black clouds had hurriedly gathered in the sky and the place would soon be getting dark. The weary gardeners knew it was going to rain heavily so decided not to leave the safety of the shelter of their temporary garden house.

As buckets of rain fell from the black sky, they knew that the gurgling yet peaceful creek that they crossed on their way to the garden would be turned into a noisy, tumbling river - big enough to carry one away if one decided to cross it at such time.

The women covered their bodies with umbrellas made from pandanus leaves, carried in their net bags, but these did not provide enough protection from the oncoming storm. Strong winds forced drops of rain from all directions towards them.

Then came hail that poured down as fine little round ice balls falling in large numbers together. It came in such a huge concentration that the banana and tanget leaves close to the gardens were broken and torn into pieces.

The cold beating down on their bodies was so severe that they were all shivering and shaking like tree branches blown around by a strong wind.

The blowing wind created a threatening whistle deep down in the valley. The sound of that whistle was terrifying to the ear as it whispered unfamiliar sounds that almost deafened their ear drums. The small group of people in the garden rushed towards each other, providing comfort and safety for one other.

As they huddled together in the small garden house, they watched in awe as the small creek close to their garden turned into a noisy, fast flowing, tumbling river as it joined the mighty Lai River. It danced and hurried on its way through the deep gorges of the whole valley, becoming a heavy torrent of somewhat fearsome and muddy water.

Pombreol

To their dismay, small pools were formed everywhere in the garden that they had just made. Going through their mind on this cold and wet evening was the fact that if the rain continued pouring down in buckets like that, all their plants will be covered by pools of water, while the freshly dug soil will be turned into mud.

Nobody wanted to say those depressing thoughts aloud as they had all worked so hard on this land. The older lady in the group was heard talking to the gods of the wind to carry the rain away, but in vain. The pelting cold rain fell until it was nearly dark.

The thunder still growled quietly up in the end of the valley but the rain had finished. Raindrops dripped from the wet trees. The only other noises were the night birds in the still air and the croaking of the frogs. The rushing of the nearby creek sounded so loud in the stillness of the fast approaching darkness.

Because the creek was flooding, the ladies stayed in the garden shelter until the high tide had slowly reduced with the ceasing rain. Pombreol and his sons picked the ladies up and walked them safely back home in the dark.

After they were all made comfortable by the warmth of the fire around the fire place, Pombreol announced that his wives and daughters were to be responsible for weeding the garden. He and his elder son were responsible for keeping the pigs out of the new garden with a strong fence to ensure a better harvest of the crops they worked so hard to plant.

Four

TRADE

After the planting, the village chief gathered his men for a meeting. He had only one agenda and that was the village festivals of feasting and dancing called the *'saida'*. As the women and children waited patiently in their homes, the men discussed the when and where and other issues of the celebration that was to take place. After the brief meeting Pombreol gathered his wives and children to disseminate the information he had received from the chief. The excited group gathered around their warrior husband and father.

Before such a feast happens, strong and able men from the village will be sent far up and down the mighty Lai River, he explained. He had gone on those journeys three times and it sure is a hell of a walk. The group suddenly went quiet. The mature people in the group knew the dangers of such trips. As for the children, they had questions to ask.

"Will your men walk up the river first or down the river first?" Nawe asked.

Pombreol

"Son, all the trips have been up the river first. After the traditional salt is exchanged for our cassowaries or bamboo oil, we will bring them here and rest for some days. Then, when we gather enough energy, we will walk down the river with some of the things we have brought from up river to exchange for bamboo oil and kina shells with those people we call the *'Her yaw'* who live far down the river," explained Pombreol.

"The bamboo oil, kina shells and other ornaments we bring from downstream, if we are lucky, will then be used for decorating our bodies for the coming feast, or be given away to the other clan's men during the celebration."

Pombreol was one of the men selected for this long journey so he gave his wives particular instructions on what to get ready for this trip. It was decided that they would start their journey in two days time. The faster, the better, so that the celebrations could take place as soon as possible.

He lifted his right hand up opening his fingers, indicating the number of days that it will take for the men to go upstream and come back. The ladies took the message. They will have to prepare raw sweet potatoes enough for that number of days.

On the morning of the journey, as each man prepared his bundle for the journey, the whole tribe gathered in front of the men's house to bid them farewell, knowing there were lots of dangers on the way. They had made enemies out of a few tribes on this route and so they would have to be extra careful. The village chief gathered them and released them with his blessing.

Pombreol was taking the family's cassowary so he would bring back enough salt and maybe a few pigs. He would take half of those traded goods down the river to the land of the Olnolokelisi and exchange that precious salt for the oil that flows from the Digaso tree. As always, his mind flew ahead of time, and he could see himself exchanging his cassowary for many lumps of salt and a few pigs. He could see how he would then take some of those goods downstream and bring not only bamboo oil collected from the Digaso tree, but also exchange his salt for kina shells and other precious ornaments that the men from that area kept for trading times like this.

The last time he went, he never bothered to ask where those kina shells and ornaments come from but this time he planned to get an answer, even if he had to make a lot of actions to express his sign language with his hands. After all, those people speak a language that nobody understands. All tribes that go there for trade usually do their business in sign language.

He suddenly woke up to reality as one of his sons gave him a gentle push. The men were leaving the village now. Each man had his bow and arrows stacked in his hand as they walked in a single straight line uphill on the narrow pathway. Nobody said anything. A few men were whistling as shortness of breath from climbing uphill overtook them.

Pombreol grabbed his possessions and joined the men. He only turned back once to wave goodbye to his family. After that he walked straight ahead as he and his men had a long way to go. This was not the time to show emotions to family or clan.

Each man walked on until they came to a sudden stop where the bush track suddenly twisted. They were about to enter the land of their worst enemy. Pombreol told them not to fear because on trading trips people were allowed access to the roads. After all, this tribe too will need to pass through their village when they want to go downstream when their turn comes.

However, if anything happened, all were asked to use their weapons and one person in the group, the fastest runner, was selected to run back for backup from their clan.

Word had been sent, through one of the woman from this village who was married into their clan, that Pombreol and the team would be passing through for their trade journey. The chief of that village had told the woman that it was a practise in the land that enemy tribes can pass through for trade purposes.

With that in mind, Pombreol led his men into the enemy's territory and walked on silently. His steps got shorter as his legs got heavier. His breathing was getting uncontrollably fast and racing with his every heartbeat - which was overtaken by the rush of adrenaline, resulting in a beat that was almost breaking his whole chest wall.

Nobody dared to say a word as they walked on. Each man could feel a paralysing fear creeping up their spine, suddenly giving them a shiver in the bright sun. Pombreol saw his men walking silently and so deliberately and thought that if their enemy attacks them right now, they would all be frozen with fear and so would be defenceless.

In the nearby undergrowth, a branch broke. All the men heard it, but nobody commented. As they walked on, there was the sound of several dry sticks breaking. Everyone stopped to look in that direction, each ready to use his arrow if need be.

As they stared in total fear, several young boys came out of their hiding place. They stared back at the strangers and ran past them loaded with mushrooms. The men lowed their bows and walked forward with much relief. These kids, they believed, were sent in to spy on them but they realised it was a genuine tribal trading journey, so they were on their way to report to their clan chief. Greatly relieved, the team continued their journey in silence, though also on the alert as they were passing through enemy land.

They were now beyond the enemy's area and stopped to drink at a nearby creek. As they walked on they came on top of a hill where all were asked to rest for a while. Each man put his bundle for trade down and rested, breathing in the fresh air. Pombreol could see the view here was beautiful and he sat there really taking it all into his mind.

As each tired man sat down to rest for a while before moving on, one of the men got up and expressed his fears as they crossed the enemy land. The rest of the men agreed, they were all grabbed by some kind of fear but it really was a relief when they saw those young boys running out of their hiding place. Pombreol then concluded that he was very thankful that the clan's chief was someone who kept his word.

The sun was already high up in the sky and they needed to move on so they again got up from their resting place and started walking again. They had to move on fast so that they could reach the camping site before dark. They walked and walked until they reached the top of the mountain that separates their land and the traditional salt people's land.

Darkness was already closing in on them so they quickly unpacked the wild dry bamboo skin and some dry wood. They laid the dry wood on top of the dry wild bamboo skin, exposing the two ends of the bamboo. One of the men stepped hard while pulling the two ends of the bamboo skin in the opposite direction. The friction and sparks caused fire to light and soon there was a huge camp fire glowing.

The warmth and heat produced by the flames was like anaesthesia to the weary travellers as they huddled around the fire. Each was struggling to absorb as much heat into his body as if to store extra for the long cold night that awaited them. As Pombreol looked around, he could see that nothing much around the camping area had changed except the camping house, which seemed to be in much need of repair. He would make sure this was repaired the next morning before they went on their way.

For now, he felt a growing sensation in his stomach and suddenly felt very hungry, so he took two pieces of his sweet potato and threw them into the fire, which was by now producing hot burning charcoal. A few other men were already enjoying their meal of roasted sweet potato over the flame of the open fire while others were lying down to rest. After his meal, Pombreol lay on the hard earth between two other men and immediately fell asleep, comforted by their body warmth. He reminded those who were still awake that they will have to repair the camping house before they continue their journey.

Early next morning Pombreol felt so cold and was thankful someone was awake and rebuilding the fire that had gone out in the night. Each man slowly got out of his sleeping place and painfully gathered around the fireplace. They had come some distance and a few men had developed muscle pain already. After a quick breakfast of roasted sweet potatoes, they helped one

Pombreol

another to quickly repair the camping house which had rotted away, and they went on their way.

As they were nearing the trading ground, someone from the group got his bamboo flute out of his bag and played a special tune. He explained to the novice that his special tune on the bamboo flute is an announcement of their presence in the land.

Suddenly men with serious faces walked out of the forest towards them. As they faced each other, nobody made any noise. All was silent until a man walked towards them with an air of authority and signalled for them to follow him. In total silence, Pombreol and his men followed him. As they walked towards wherever they were being led to, Pombreol was getting uncomfortable with the silence, as well as the weight of his bundle for the exchange. He was perspiring from the weight of his possessions as well as a strange feeling of being away from home, being in a strange place with strange men who even spoke strange languages.

He wondered why it was not the same man who knew a bit of their language who was the one leading them to their chief. This one was a younger man and obviously, he didn't know Pombreol and his clan's language too. This trade was going to be difficult. As they were led to the chief, each man greeted the other by the shake of his hand and was welcomed by the village chief. Pombreol gave a sigh of relief. They were given shelter and food. The trade was taking place the next morning.

The next day, Pombreol and his men presented their goods before the men from that village, who exchanged them for lumps of salt and pigs from their area. Pombreol exchanged a female pig for his cassowary and a lump of traditional salt from that land. He would take some of the salt downstream to further exchange for other goods.

Pombreol

With much negotiation, resulting in trading of goods with each other, Pombreol and his men thanked the chief of the village for his hospitality and kindness and left the village at noon time. After a night of resting at their camp site, they arrived back in their own village with their bundle of goods.

The village chief and the rest of the family members were all glad to see their men coming home safely and bringing what they went for. They were given five days to rest. After that, they would be going downstream for the precious bamboo oil, kina shells and other valuable ornaments that can only come from the land downstream, where the very tiny people called the 'Heyo' live.

After sufficient rest and regaining their strength, each man again gathered his extra goods for trade and left for the next trade grounds. The chief bid them a safe trip and wished them luck. Going downstream for trade was a lot easier as they had no enemy tribe on the way.

However, they were somewhat fearful of the trading ground with its people. Their elders always pointed out that this happens because when people die, their spirit follows the rivers downstream. That is why the people from downstream look the way they do.

As they walked down, Pombreol remembered what he told his wives and children. He told them that the journey he was taking was far too dangerous therefore, "Keep your eyes on that banana tree in front of your house. The young shoot of that banana is about to fall off its tip to bear fruit. If it falls towards the sunrise, know that I may not be coming home. However, if it falls towards the west then, be assured, I will be coming back to you my wives and children safe and sound." At those words his wives and children wept openly.

He remembered how much control he had to put up as he fought back tears. His wife, now a few months pregnant, was putting her hands on her head and crying. She was tearing his heart apart but he had to go for this trade trip as it was important.

The things needed to declare them wealthy came from those far away lands and he wouldn't let the opportunity pass. Not even for his children or his pregnant wife. He was willing to jeopardise his own life and his family's welfare for this particular trade route. He gave a sudden shiver as he recalled the frightening events that had taken place for some traders. Stories about how some men from the other side of the mountain went missing on this trade route were common in the area. He was sure this was the most dangerous and frightening trade route for his tribesmen.

However, he also knew that without the goods exchanged on this journey, his clan would never be recognised and accepted as an able and rich clan. They would not reach certain levels of achievement if much needed ornaments and bamboo oil for the *saida* celebration were not available.

Realising that the men had already walked ahead and were leaving him behind, he quickly picked up his pace in order to reach them. After climbing high mountains, then down into yet another valley, and sometimes battling up sheer cliffs of rock, they walked on, most of the time in silence, as each man concentrated on this most dangerous walk. They walked miles and miles until they reached the swinging bridge by which they were to cross the wide swirling rivers. The men kept walking through the narrow, rough and muddy native track until they reached their destination.

Pombreol

The men of that land of Digaso oil and other precious goods also had to walk some distance to meet them, so that trading happened at a central location. They knew their trading days so would make themselves available at the time set. As they approached the usual trading area, Pombreol could see that the other men were quietly staring at them suspiciously. They may have just arrived since a few other men were lying down as if to rest their weary bodies.

Pombreol lifted his hands up as the sign of the peaceful greeting and their leader also lifted his hands up to return his peaceful greetings. After each man rested for a while, cooling themselves with cold water and sweet potatoes leftovers from the morning breakfast, they all agreed to start their business straight away.

Goods were carefully and proudly fully displayed as usual, and Pombreol and his men examined each ornament carefully to make sure none was damaged or cracked. They also examined them to make sure every item of goods was in excellent form and no fault was to be found.

This process took quite some time as the Heyo people silently stared at them suspiciously. After examining carefully all the goods from both sides, and being fully satisfied with the value and durability of the ornaments, the men allowed exchange to take place.

After that the bamboo oil from the Digaso tree was traded. Pombreol got himself a bamboo of oil and several kina shells and a few other ornaments. When both parties were satisfied with their trade, each man carried his load and walked slowly back to their camping site. Each man watched his back to make sure nobody was making any negative move at another.

When Pombreol was sure the trade had turned out well and the Heyo men were walking satisfactorily away with the goods that he and his tribesmen had brought, he also walked with his men slowly back up the hill in order to get to the camp site as soon as possible. It would be another burden for the men to walk in the dark with their load of goods.

The final light of the sun has just disappeared over the hilltop and darkness was fast closing in on them as they reached their campsite. Each man safely stored his precious goods away and immediately fell asleep on the warm hard earth, only made comfortable and warm by the glowing camp fire and warmth and comfort of each other's body.

Someone was heard thanking the gods for this trade that did not go sour. This was all on their mind but they were too weary to make a lot of comment, and immediately fell asleep. The strange night noises from this unfamiliar land were like a fading dream as each man gave way to his weariness and fell into a deep sleep, totally exhausted.

They were all awake just before the sun rose. Each man quickly gathered his load and they made their way home in the early hours of the morning, all wanting to climb the hill before the sun rose. The wind had swept the sky clear of the thick black clouds, and the big, glistening morning star hung motionless in the east. Each man shook off the tiredness from his sleepy eyes, gathered his precious possessions, and hurriedly walked up the steep hill.

As they reached the top of the mountain that overlooked the valley, the morning sun had woken up, brightening the entire eastern sky. Its beautiful rays were spreading quickly across to where the travellers stood silently watching the event that was unfolding before them. Today promised to be a perfect day. Standing together they looked down the valley; the darkness they left behind was now looking for a place to hide. They breathed in the cold air deeply, and turned their backs on the whole valley to face their road ahead.

A clump of trees on their right sheltered them from the cold breeze that swept down the mountain ranges at the end of the valley. Through the gaps in the trees, they could see a thick, white mist at the foothills of the stern mountains. The path now curved away, rolling gently, sometimes sloping steeply, to the opposite hills. As they walked on, rugged mountains, purple and grey in the dawn, seemed to stand like armed warriors encircling the sleeping valley, providing security and protection for its people. It was a journey never to be forgotten.

After five days of their most dangerous journey, Pombreol and his men arrived safely back in their village. The village chief had been sitting anxiously at the village entrance. When he saw the weary travellers arriving, he started running towards them and the whole village followed suit. Pombreol took his goods home, where his family told him that the banana fell to the western side so they already knew that he would be safe.

Later, in the afternoon, there was a big feast to celebrate the safe trading of goods both upstream and downstream. Each man was proud of what he had brought home. The gods were in favour of Pombreol and his clansmen as they did not face any dangers or problems on the journey. So they celebrated with great joy.

Five

SINGSING & PIG KILL

Pombreol and his clansmen rested for a few days after the long journey. Every man who went for the trade needed that rest badly. Pombreol developed bilateral knee swelling while a few other men complained of painful thighs from the overuse of their legs from miles and miles of walking. One novice on the journey had all his muscles smashed up like smashed up potatoes. They applied special bush leaves to erase their pain and receive fast healing.

After that, the chief of the village gathered the whole clan. There really was no time to be wasted as they had preparation to do in anticipation for the great day. It was time to plan for the much anticipated singsing and the big pig kills after the singsing. He announced to the gathered people his intention to get plans going for the most important celebration of any clan in the area. As the discussion went on and on, excited kids played around while the men spoke what was on their mind.

Pombreol

Pombreol, in summing it all up, announced to the clan that in two months time the celebration will start and, as of the following day, each man was asked to get firewood, stones, leaves and ferns ready for the pig kill. After all that was ready, every man and woman who was taking part in the singsing will look for materials far and near to decorate their body. Everybody walked back to their dwelling place with heads held high as they thought about their celebration and the coming big event.

In the men's dwelling hut, discussion continued and everyone was talking, sometimes above each other's voices, as they excitedly discussed about how huge and how many pigs they were killing. The discussion further continued with who was going to be decorated for the dancing. Pombreol and his men decided that whoever wants to decorate themselves can do so as long as they have all decoration materials available. Soon all the discussion faded away and the men fell asleep, while a few whispered to each other about the special event that was coming up.

Early the following morning, Pombreol called his young sons together. With a few raw sweet potatoes meant for his breakfast, each started walking up to the riverside to chop down a big, dry tree to cut up for the pig kill. They worked hard the whole day, chopping and splitting the dry wood. The bang, bang, bang sound of the stone axe against the wood was the only noise in the silent forest while the men worked in silence with sweat pouring down their bare brown bodies in the cool of the day. Stopping briefly only for a drink or lunch of roasted sweet potato, they worked till late.

After all the pieces of log were split for use as firewood during the feast, each man carried one on his shoulder and walked slowly home. They decided that the rest of the split firewood could be carried up in the days to come. For now, their poor bodies were in so much pain and agony, they needed to rest.

In the men's hut, they huddled around the fireplace and, with the day's events tiring their bodies, quietly walked to their sleeping place and immediately fell asleep as tiredness overtook their weary eyes.

Pombreol lay down beside his son Nawe but could only stay awake as his mind ran through which pig to kill and how many would fit the number of people he was inviting. He also ran through his mind which men he would select for the operation of all his pigs. He continued to count in his mind how many pigs he would kill. He wanted to kill twenty four pigs, because twenty four was the last number in their counting system and his upcoming leadership ability would be recognised if he killed this number, or a number beyond that.

In his mind, he continued to count the number of pigs his wives had in his pig pen. To his dismay, he realised his three wives were looking after six pigs each only, so he must borrow pigs from some other relatives from another clan and repay them later. He was still trying to work things out when a sudden heaviness overtook his eyes and he immediately fell asleep.

At the sound of the first morning bird, each man was awake to continue their work in the preparation for the big event. In the ladies' house, the women were awake before daylight and had prepared breakfast for their family.

Pombreol gathered his wives and children and told them about his plans to kill twenty four or more pigs. Before he even completed his speech, one of his wives

Pombreol

said they had only 18 pigs in the family and she definitely was not releasing all of hers. Pombreol simply told her all the pigs in his household will be slaughtered and that's it. Women like you have no choice but to listen and obey!

The ladies including the one who spoke her mind couldn't say anything now because they would be asking for trouble. Pombreol then told all three ladies to go to their parents and brothers and ask them for two or more pigs. "Tell them our husband needs more pigs to kill for the coming event and their pigs will be repaid later," he told them. He and his sons would continue with what they had started yesterday.

They worked hard the whole day, only stopping for a drink or lunch. Later that evening they were all so tired but were satisfied their firewood work was completed.

That evening, all three ladies were home with different stories. The first lady told her husband, her brothers gave her four pigs and she was told to collect them when ready to be killed. The second one, the rebellious one, announced that her relatives told her they had given enough pigs to her, most of which were never repaid, so they can't give any now. As for the third and younger wife, her brothers gave her two pigs and they will bring them the day before the actual killing.

Pombreol was furious with the second wife for not securing any pigs from her relatives and he told her so. However the woman, with her irritating manner, only talked back at him. Pombreol asked her how many pigs he owed her brothers and she screamed that ten pigs had been borrowed for various activities.

Pombreol knew this lady was just covering up for her lazy and poor brothers who never knew how to look

Pombreol

after pigs but were just good at talking, and he told her so. She replied that he was a dog himself if he had no pig to kill and was begging from her brothers.

At that Pombreol got a big stick and belted her like never before. He ordered her to leave his household and go back to her brothers. "You good for nothing, leave my area and never return," he told her.

She replied that she had six pigs and will kill them in this feast because she had a son and she didn't want other women to laugh at her for deserting her son and going away on special times like this event. "Otherwise, I could leave with all of my pigs you must know," she said.

"Which pigs are you referring to?" asked Pombreol. "Did they come from your lazy good for nothing brothers? They are wealth from my own household. As for your brothers, they can give you nothing but only their pubic hair," he screamed, and belted her some more. After beating her up, he shouted some more aggressive words and went back to the men's hut.

In the ladies house, everyone gathered around the badly beaten wife to assess how many injuries she had sustained. One of the daughters was advised to bring in leaves from outside. They were warmed over the open fire and the hot leaves applied over the bruises and other painful areas.

The next day, Pombreol gathered his wives and children and told them that the *mumu* stones they had were not enough for the number of pigs about to be slaughtered. Therefore the activity for the days to come was to collect stones from the river and gather them at their *mumu* site. All except for the beaten wife, who was nursing her wounds in the house, worked tirelessly to gather the stones. They all knew that they had to have enough stones or the pigs won't be cooked well.

Bystanders saw the amount of stones lined up on Pombreol's *mumu* ground and word spread around that Pombreol was killing a great number of pigs. Such words brought pride into his heart and Pombreol would walk around the village always driving his family to work hard.

All the things needed for the feast were gathered and the gathering place was full to its capacity now. Final touches were going on and Pombreol was overjoyed that his younger sister Hubin, who was married to a distant villager, had brought her two huge pigs. She told him one of the pigs was to repay his pig she and her husband had borrowed, and the other one was to help him in this event. He was killing twenty six pigs in total. No wonder people were whispering his name among those with the highest number of pigs to kill.

Everyone was told to gather their resources for those who were taking part in the singsong and dancing to decorate their bodies. This would take place before the actual pig kill. Men from other clans were also invited for the singsing and dancing and three other clans had already notified their intention to take part in the dancing.

There was an atmosphere of pure excitement in the village; everybody gathered body decoration stuff from the bush. Those who did not own body decoration ornaments would borrow from others. Hiring of precious bird of paradise feathers and other head dress ornaments was not forgotten as well. In the ladies' long house, grass skirts were woven. Other precious items such as belts to be worn around the waist on top of the grass skirt were sought, borrowed or hired and prepared to be worn on that day.

On the final day of preparation, boys went to the mountain to get the special leaves that grow in the thick forest, to cover their bottoms. The leaves will sway up and down as the men dance to the beat of their kundu drums. The elders have already told them the importance of those things as there will be people looking at them and they will be judged accordingly as the other two rival clans are also taking part in the singsing and dancing.

That afternoon excitement in the village was felt like never before. New faces could be seen everywhere as guests from far and near arrived. In Pombreol's house, his sister Hubin and her relatives had arrived the day before and so she was now giving a helping hand in the preparation of everything. His mother's relatives from over the mountain had also arrived. It was surely getting crowded fast!

Pombreol and the chief gathered the people to make sure all preparations were up to date and that nobody was lacking in anything. The chief's youngest daughter and another girl were selected to lead the singsing and dancing groups coming from nearby rival areas. This was how men coming into other men's village were made welcome. The two girls will have to meet them at the entrance of their gathering place and lead them in dancing into the main singsing area.

The chief also announced that if some of their clan members did not have some materials needed for the decoration of their body, the others who have them must share with them, to which everybody nodded in agreement.

Pombreol

Out in the men's hut, it was so crowded and hot. Pombreol wanted to walk out again and get some fresh air but knew he couldn't - there was a long day ahead and he needed to rest. However, this was not to be - the noise increased and increased until there was noise everywhere as men talked about the dancing and celebration that was to be held.

Pombreol then took the time to think about who to share his bamboo oil and a few other ornaments he had brought from the trade exchange with. In his mind he continued to count who he had invited for the pig kill and just remembered a few of his most important friends. He will have to send word the next day. After all, the day was hectic and he just didn't have the time to even sit down and breath.

Some time later, the fire in the fireplace had slowly glowed down and men were heard snoring away softly in their own corners. Pombreol fell asleep immediately.

By very early the next morning almost everyone in the village was wide awake. Body decoration stuff was brought out from their hiding places and people who were taking part in the dancing were decorated, done by just a few people who were allocated the job. The others watched on with admiration.

Still others just walked from one decorated group to another giving their opinion and views of how they should be decorated. Some were also helping to give a hand on other bits and pieces that aid in full completion of the body decorations. Sometimes the comments were helpful while other times it was just irritating. When it was irritating, one could hear people swearing at each other. Nobody minded about it as the great day had arrived and excitement itself was really brewing up.

Faces were painted and a variety of splendid headdresses made up of Bird of Paradise feathers were worn on top of wigs made from their own hair. Bodies were smeared with special coloured mud from the rivers. Ladies wore woven grass skirts while men wore aprons made of traditional strings in front while their special leaves were worn at the back.

Kina shells painted with extremely rare bright red dye were worn in front. Pectoral ornaments made of larger mother of pearl pieces cut into shape, hanging from a necklace that passed over the head freely, were also worn. Bodies were also rubbed with the bamboo oil brought in by trade. Leaves worn by men to cover up their buttocks were also rubbed with oil.

Other body ornaments and ritual objects were also worn to complete their body decorations, so judges could not find even the smallest mistake in their ruling of the best decorated person. These extra objects were mainly animal materials like pig tusks, cuscus skin and fur, and feathers from different species of birds.

The sun had now spread over the whole valley and soon the land was getting warm with the heat of the sun as well as the excitement of the people. Commentators and other elders were now asking the people to speed up with their decorations as this festival of celebration of the ancient ways was going to take time to judge, and time was catching up.

Hundreds of people in the valley could not come to the big dance because they were enemies of Pombreol and his clan's men.

The two young girls who were selected to lead the singsing and welcome the other singsing groups were led by the commentators to the entrance of the village and were asked to wait. One of the young girls then realised that the tail of the cuscus which was to be worn at the back of her head was nowhere to be found. They search everywhere but were unable to locate it. Luckly, the daughter of the chief had two so she allowed the girl to borrow the one that she wasn't using.

Pombreol and his tribesmen gathered in the middle of the ceremonial ground. His clan's ceremonial ground was on top of a hill and was very flat, pretty well surrounded by very tall and graceful Casuarina trees growing very closely together, planted by the men. In the centre of their ceremonial ground was an earth mound on top of which three very tall casuarina trees thrust their heads up into the sky.

Pombreol and his men marched up to the ceremonial grounds to start their singing and dancing. The two decorated girls stood tall with pride at the entrance into the clan's ceremonial grounds, ready to welcome the men from the rival but friendly clan who were taking part in the day's event. As the men sang their songs in the very loudest and throatiest voices they could muster, they danced to the rhythm of their kundu drums. Songs from the other tribes in response were heard as they also marched towards the main singing place. More songs were sung as the excitement grew thick.

There were quick rushes of movement by bystanders as the crowd was controlled by the few men who were tasked to do that job. The rival singing group was marching into the village and the two girls at the gate had taken their place as they led the men into the ceremonial ground. They would lead the dance around the mound in the centre of the ceremonial grounds four times until the men took their permanent position for the celebrations for the rest of the day.

These two girls were selected to lead the parade for their innocent and undisturbed beauty, looks and style of dance. The two girls danced backwards, facing the parade, as they led the men into their own ceremonial ground. All were focused on the two girls as they moved and danced together in unity and one motion, dancing to the melody of the beating of the kundu. Their beautiful bodies also swayed gracefully to the melody of the dancing songs sung by the dancing men they were leading.

This was the time when the married and elderly ladies recalled memories of their time and talked among themselves, refreshing old memories. The beating of the kundu drum and the songs that were sung by the dancers accelerated their poor hearts to beat at a rate that was not really healthy for some! But they couldn't help it as the words of the songs and the chants of the dancers had special meaning in their hearts.

The atmosphere was quickly growing thick with great excitement as three different clans marched in and the two girls led them. They then marched around four times and took their positions each in an orderly fashion. As they took their places and sang and danced to the beat of the kundu drums, decorated women from rival clans were placed in between two men so they could all dance together. These two men were either the girl's boyfriend or a relative of the boyfriend.

Judges then went around giving their judgment on which clan was best dressed or which individual man or a woman was dressed the best. They also commented on who was giving the best performance with their best style of dance.

Every tribe had their own signature looks and their own special moves. Even the song they sang had special words as each clan recalled mountains or rivers from their own village in the words of their songs.

Soon the dancing was into full swing. Young and old alike were taken in by the harmonising rhythm of the kundu drums and the crescendo of the dancing men singing in unison. Nothing can stir up the blood more than simply hearing the chorus of voices rising and falling in unison, in response to the commanding pace of the kundu. This had specific meanings and messages for the people it was meant for.

For the old men and women, memories of their golden times locked up somewhere in their mind were somehow refreshed by the sound of the chanted songs, while the young people enjoyed the moment anyway. This gathering was one of the biggest as there were more tribes decked out in all their glory, singing and dancing and waving their weapons.

As Pombreol danced away, two of the women from the other clans had taken both of his sides to dance with him. The lady on his left side had looked so cool with her decorations that several people had come to tie her fingers with ropes so that, later in the day, she would have to pay the owners of the ropes with wealth to untie those ropes.

As the sun was pointing towards the east, the time had come for undecorated people to perform the final part of the celebrations. As far as all were concerned, this was the most enjoyable part of the whole ceremonial performances and processes. This time restless young men and women formed several big circles for the end of the day's performance, called the *'waipa'*.

As the *waipa* melody rose up and down, the young men and women danced around in circles. Even the decorated men formed their own circles and joined in the *waipa* rhythm.

More and more groups of large circles were formed by the ladies in their own ethnic groups and their tunes of chanted songs were heard in several different directions. The place was noisy with the songs from the *waipa* and the women's tunes; yet the noises were not overpowering each other. Somehow, all the different tunes blended into a unified melody in the cold air. It was a day of pure excitement and enjoyment.

As the sun was driving towards the far east, two of the groups of women's songs were building up to their extreme. One could hear from the words of the song that they were fighting for a man.

As the songs got more aggressive, with the use of extreme profane language aimed at each other in the words of their song, the two rival groups were joined in by mature women from their own sides to build in more heat.

The boy they were fighting for was identified as the son of the chief of the village. Pombreol felt that severe fighting among the ladies would evolve if nothing was done, so he asked the chief to make a decision on one of the women for his son. The reply was that both can be paid bride price at the same time as one was the boy's choice and the other lady was his choice. This decision was made known to the ladies and the two groups walked away in peace.

Courting night among the young people was set for the night that was approaching fast. Among them were young boys who were allowed to take part in the very thrilling dance, talking about it to the others who were not allowed to join in while they dropped off to sleep.

Pombreol

As the crowd slowly got smaller, those remaining were from Pombreol's village, or from far away villages invited for the feast the next day. In the men's house, all the talk was about the day's event and the feast next day. The noise was too much but it all faded in Pombreol's mind as he remembered the woman who was dancing on his right side. She was pretty indeed. He would give this homework of investigating her background to one of the men in the morning. He did his best to look for her in the crowd but she had disappeared. The thought of her brought a smile, but the day's event had exhausted him so much that he fell asleep.

His dreams were all for this decorated short but beautiful women by his side. She was swaying her body so peacefully that he stood transfixed to the spot and stared at her as if he had never seen a woman in his life.

Someone coughing very close to his ear woke him up suddenly. He could see daylight was fast approaching and he had a long day ahead so he slowly sat up to plan and start his activities. Somewhere nearby in one of the ladies' houses, he could hear the *tumen* in final stage as daylight was fast approaching.

He woke up the men in the house as he knew they all had a long day ahead - they had a lot of pigs to be killed and slaughtered for the feast. As the pigs were killed and the hair burned and cleaned out, Pombreol got men who were his invited guests to butcher them up. All the intestines were given to the women to clean while the men prepared the rest of the pigs for the *mumu*. The women took them to the river and cleaned everything up.

As more people arrived for the feast, there were people everywhere. Pieces of pork were being roasted on the open fire and eaten. One could really feel that the

Pombreol

feast was being enjoyed by the people and the day was going to be an enjoyable and memorable day.

Pombreol gathered all his pigs' internal organs and started to share them among his guests. He gave them all a piece each until all his guests had some raw meat to cook and eat while waiting for the main pieces, which will be taken home to share with the rest of the family.

Men and young boys lined dry firewood up in the long trenches prepared for the *mumu*. They started to make fires, heating up the stones which were laid on top of the firewood. After the stones were heated up, the big final *mumu* was now in progress.

Each man knew exactly where to *mumu* his own pig so nothing was mixed up or lost. After the *mumu* was done, the cooked pigs were cut into pieces and shared among friends, relatives and guests. Stuffed pig's stomach was given to the young girls of eligible courting age to give to their boyfriends, making their courting official.

Pombreol knew this was one of the biggest pig kills and was proud of himself for killing a great number of pigs and achieving one of his dreams.

But all things must come to an end. Great masses of grey storm clouds rolled in from the northern end of the valley, and the thunder began to rumble threateningly. All the people gathered their share of pork and hurried off home.

Next day everybody thought the celebrations were one of the largest and they had enjoyed them to the fullest. Even the very old people down to the youngest enjoyed it like there was no tomorrow.

However, Pombreol still must look for that mysterious short girl who swayed her body so smoothly and attractively beside him, following the beat of his kundu drum and dancing in union with him as if they were one.

Pombreol

He now recalled how he danced to every beat for her. His heart had somehow gone out of control and started beating at a pace that he never thought would be possible. He just turned in her direction to ask for her name when, to his surprise, he realised she had slipped out and disappeared the way she came. He was so disappointed he had been too carried away trying to control his heart beat as well as the kundu drum when she sneaked off. He smiled to himself as he planned how he would look for her and make her his wife.

After all he was already a wealthy and prominent man and needed to add more wives to his household. What girl wouldn't want him for a husband, with the way he was rising so fast in the society?

Six

RITUAL INITIATION INTO ADULTHOOD

As the days went by, Pombreol's third wife was in her final stage of pregnancy. It was around this time that Pombreol and his tribesmen needed to go out into the forest to leave their young boys for their final initiation into adulthood.

The boys who were to go for the final testing were the ones who had passed the first two tests. That is, they had built a perfect highlands round house all by themselves from the start of full moon until the next full moon, and they had cleared and planted a big hectare of land within a certain number of full moons, as set by the village elders.

There were nine boys who went through the initiation but five had failed. Only four had managed it. These four were ready to be taken for their final test while the rest had to start all over again.

This final initiation process was for the participants to be separated from the women folk and be segrated for a period of up to five full moons while they learned the process of masculinisation. This was nothing hard except they had to stay a long time away from home in the forest where a special group of men used magic and special ingredients to grow and shape the boy's hair before it was clipped off and used as a ceremonial wig.

There was lots of activity going on in the village as the tribesmen prepared for a day's trip to the mountains. The boys would be left there for five full moons to grow their hair long and thick, without returning to the village. This process was known as the 'Iri ip Kale'. The two specialists for this initiation also got their magic stuff and the ingredients for the hair growth ready for the trip.

The food for their hair would be thick pig's fat, left in the young boys hair, which melts away gradually, nourishing and smoothing their hair so it grows thick, heavy and long. This would identify the boys move from boyhood to adulthood, after which they were ready for courtship then marriage.

The fat was now bundled and carried by the men of the village. Stacks and stacks of pig fat bundles were carried as heaps would be needed for the ceremony. With the bundled-up fat in banana leaves on their shoulders, Pombreol and his men walked and walked until they arrived at the campsite.

The sun had already set over the high mountains and night animals were heard singing their nightly chorus from far and near, sounding creepy in the dark. But none of the weary travellers seemed to mind as a huge weariness had fallen over them from the whole day's walk. They quickly made their campfire and roasted their sweet potatoes over the fire, ate a quick meal and prepared a place to rest. Darkness was closing in on them faster than would have happened in the village. Each man quickly settled in for the night, laying down his wearied body on the hard ground around the fireplace. At least the fire glowing in the dark was a comfort as the dense forest didn't seem as friendly as it was during day.

This time the huge trees of the forest, which now looked like giants dwarfing over them, seemed to be staring in an unfriendly way down at them. The undergrowth seemed to be whispering to itself in a wicked way, as if the humans were intruding and were not going to be treated as guests.

The forest animals were not any more friendly either as their noise was getting louder, as if angry about something. What would they be so angry about? A few of the men felt a chill run up their spine but none spoke out for fear of being laughed at in the morning.

Each man huddled around the fireplace as the glowing light in the total darkness and the feel of each other's body provided some comfort, helping maintain some heat in their bare skin in the cold air.

As Pombreol lay there on his makeshift bed listening to the night noise, his mind went off to the last time he had come around this way. It was a rainy day when he and five other boys were to be left behind. At that time, he felt like he was being led to his very death as the men who led them seemed to be so serious. And the silence was so uncomfortable as those men looked fearsome and walked in total silence, always stopping to take a little rest. He tried to make some attempt at conversation but they all seemed not interested so he had given up and joined the silence. It really wasn't easy getting into adult society.

Pombreol

Laying there on the hard earth with a few leaves spread under him as his bed, he remembered how hard it had been for him as he tried to build that house all by himself. Painfully he remembered how long it took for his stone axe, handed down to him from his father, to cut down the trees for his house and also to clear the land to make the garden.

He moved uncomfortably on the rough bed which was rapidly causing a sore back from the cold hard ground and the freezing mountain air. He then recalled the blisters and red raw hands. But in those days he couldn't complain because the elders were always there with hard, emotionless faces.

He had almost broken down, but he didn't want to go through it again as he knew it wouldn't be any easier later. Therefore he had carried on until he had passed it all and the elders had approved - with some wicked grins. At least those faces were not hard forever.

Growing hair or the 'Iri ip Kale' period wasn't bad for him. His father had killed the biggest pig. It was the most special day in his life for he was leaving boyhood behind and would be a man after he had grown his hair. He had rested with the boys in the bush until they were due to present themselves before the village elders.

Nobody was allowed to see or visit them. If they were seen, the whole ritual would be broken. Therefore only men who had no wives were allowed to take them their food supply and extra pig's fat for their hair growth.

He could remember how an old bachelor in the village would bring in their supplies. He would store extra supplies for them in a hollow of a big tree and walk back to the village alone. With a sudden sadness

Pombreol thought of this very kind man who had left this world earlier and gone to be with the ancestors.

With those thoughts still on his mind he fell asleep with his bows and arrows at his side. Somewhere there in the dark thick forest, he heard an owl hooting away, but he faded away in his dreams.

Seven

DEATH, CAUSES & AFTERLIFE

Early next morning the tribesmen left the boys, after giving them direction to their final destination, and returned to the village by the same route. As they walked home, most of the time in silence, a messenger bird called a *'mondil'* was heard singing somewhere in the thick bush and they knew there was sad news waiting for them in the village, for this kind of song was a bad omen. Pombreol also thought of the owl he had heard last night and he walked home with a heavy heart. The owl sang funeral songs only and that knowledge was common in the land.

Nearing the village they heard an uproar of noise. As they got closer the noise sounded like funeral cries. Knowing that someone had died, they all hurried forward with heavy hearts.

When they were in the clearing at the top of the hill they could see a crowd of people outside Pombreol's house. All moved faster except Pombreol, who stood transfixed to the ground, wondering who in his young family would have left so early, for nobody was sick when he left.

Pombreol

Did the magician from the enemy tribe perform his witchcraft aiming for him but got someone else because he wasn't around? Yes, that could be the explanation for the fierce wild winds which were blowing the other night when they were about to leave for the trip. Most of the trees in the village were uprooted and a few food gardens destroyed.

Whoever it was, he had to go and find out first before even thinking of the cause of death. However, he was rooted to the spot for fear of the news. After all, he was always proud of his family and didn't want anyone dead. Even that unwanted woman was part of his life already as she mothered her son. His heart was beating very fast against his chest and he was almost out of breath for fear of the news.

He could see someone racing towards him as he walked down. It didn't look like an adult and yes, that was Nawe, he could recognize him from afar by the way he slightly threw his leg to the side when he ran. Oh, what a relief, for he could not put up with the grief of losing his first born since first sons are meant to take their father's place.

Nawe was already beside him talking between breaths. "Father, my third mother died inside that small house and ladies brought her out."

He couldn't believe it. How could that be? She was doing fine when he left. He was now overcome with grief, for this was his younger wife and she died particularly because of him; the magic meant for him got her while he was away.

He started weeping so loudly, his son stopped talking and started crying with him. His wailing got louder when he saw her lifeless form. He cried more bitterly

Pombreol

when he saw her swollen tummy, knowing his baby was still trapped inside.

The gathering people wept as a few ladies changed their tone of cry and started chanting special mourning songs for their lady friend. More tears flowed freely from the eyes of those who were attending the funeral.

After people rested from mourning Pombreol was told that she was having difficulty in delivering her child for one shoulder was coming out first. She tried to push the baby out but the child refused to come out. She tried and tried until she fell down dead not long ago today with the baby still inside. She was actually in pain when they left the village but how could he know? Those were the things of a woman. The old woman who helped such mothers tried to pull the arm out but the baby didn't want to come out.

Just before she died his wife was heard calling her grandmother's name, so whispers were that her grandmother had an unsolved disagreement with her mother, so her spirit was keeping the unborn baby inside, killing her.

In the silence of the funeral, a child was heard asking its mother where had she gone to? The mother drew her child closer to herself and whispered into the ear that she had gone to the bad spirits' place down the south end. She was now an evil spirit who will go about eating people by making them sick, leading to death.

But why should she eat any one of us, after all we all loved her? The mother told him to shut up as people are not allowed to talk too much during a funeral ceremony. The child immediately shut his mouth and was never heard asking further questions again.

Pombreol too wondered why someone as loving as his dear wife would turn into a bad spirit and eat them. He couldn't accept that but because this was the teaching from his old people, he was forced to accept it.

For now, he felt relief as he realized that he was not to be blamed for the death of his young wife. After all, she was only a young woman. What could possibly cause her death? It had to be that old woman's spirit only. Whatever the cause, it would have to be discussed later. For now he had pressing and important matters to talk about.

Right now, all his bride price would be returned since she had died without even giving him a child, and her own grandmother happened to be the cause of his wife and infant's death. If they weren't able to repay the price, they would have to give him a new bride as her replacement.

After her burial in the traditional cemetery, the whole village gathered to discuss the funeral feast and a few other issues surrounding the death of this young woman. A day was selected for the feast and a few men were selected to guard the burial ground in the night for fear of *sanguma* women, who usually turn into a dog to come for the corpse.

Pombreol and his cousins were among the men selected. They sat hidden by some tall grass, leaving enough space to see the burial area. The moon was late in coming up therefore it was quite dark. Two other boys were sitting in different areas with their bows and arrows ready to shoot anything that moved near the freshly dug area.

Pombreol thought he saw a movement but he wasn't too sure, so he waited. After waiting for a while and just about the time they were giving up, there was a movement and a black dog approached the burial area.

Pombreol

Pombreol felt himself shivering not from the cold but from fear.

He was almost shaking when his cousin pinched him so hard that he tasted blood as he bit his lips together to stop himself from crying out. As he got his arrow ready there was a strike somewhere and the dog was seen jumping up in the air in the bright moonlight. So someone else had seen the dog first.

As he was about to relax the dog ran towards him. Pombreol shot the dog right through the eye with his arrow, but the dog kept running. The guards gathered together and whispered among themselves that this was no ordinary dog as it never once cried with pain like any normal and real dog would do. They also concluded that there was no dog similar to this particular one in their village. With a heavy sigh, Pombreol knew the night guard was not wasted, someone was bound to die and that person was the one who had transformed themself into the very dog they had just shot.

The next day they heard cries in the village downstream and knew it was the witch or saguma woman who had turned herself into a dog and was killed at the ceremony. Pombreol and his men congratulated themselves for guarding his wife's graveyard well and killing the most feared witch in the area.

The men from her village, too, were happy because this one woman was also the cause of many deaths in their village recently. They had always wanted to eliminate her but no opportunity had been found until this time, when she was seeking the dead body to feast on. Her death meant people would be roasting their pork and other animal meat with its special aroma hanging freely in the air without the fear of the special burning and smoking scent attracting the witch, who would bewitch one of the family members to death. It was a great relief for the whole community as they would not be living in fear anymore.

A week after Pombreol's third wife's burial, the clansmen gathered to find out the person who had caused the death. Before she was buried, the village chief had ordered one of the women to cut off some of the dead woman's hair and finger nails, which were then kept by the chief. These were then brought out to the open and wrapped up in dry banana leaves. The bundle was tied onto a piece of bamboo. As the people gathered and watched in fear, the village chief called the name of the dead woman, at the same time talking to the bamboo with its possessions.

"Take the bamboo to the person who has caused your death. If that person is dead, then take them to the next of kin," he said.

As soon as the chief had finished his ceremony, the bamboo with its procession started moving spontaneously. More words were spoken to it which seemed to make the movement faster. While that was going on, two of the strongest men of the tribe were selected to hold each end of the piece of bamboo.

After the two men each took their end of the bamboo, the people watched wide eyed as it moved, leading them to areas the woman had been to within the last twenty four hours before her death. The two men followed without stopping as the bamboo moved faster and faster, leading them further on. An unseen force was certainly moving the bamboo, which made a few people shiver too!

Pombreol

Pombreol waited anxiously in the village for this was the time to know the truth. The sun was setting and the bamboo hadn't landed on anybody yet but still swung faster and faster, quickly exhausting the two men.

Feeling exhausted, the people gave up following around and decided to wait at the village. If it had landed on someone they would know about it anyway. Two other men tried to replace the first two but the bamboo couldn't move, therefore they continued.

After the two men almost collapsed from exhaustion, the bamboo finally landed on the dead grandmother's last daughter and wouldn't move anymore. The young woman sat silently with sweat dripping down in the cool evening. As the silence grew, a big night bird was heard singing in the distance and a few shivered as the night drew near.

The village chiefs of both villages quickly decided that the cause of death was on her own side of the family therefore all the bride price would be refunded since she hadn't even left a child for Pombreol. After all, women were brought to bear children and this was not to be. Having solved that, the people went back to their houses, talking among themselves about the recent events and the soon coming funeral feast.

In the night, Pombreol was having dinner with his wives when rain started pouring down. The younger children gathered around their father as this was one of his rare times to spend with his wives and children.

As the rain got heavier, there was a strong cold wind which blew the rain wildly against the house. The vivid sheets of lightening were terrifying and the children, frightened by the thunder, huddled closely against their father. Young Porenong was always frightened of thunder so she snuggled very close to Pombreol and asked him what the thunder meant, and what the lightening was all about.

"Well my child," he began, "high up in the sky lives the spirit men and women called the Yegi. When they talk and argue, thunder is their voices, while the lightening is the arrow they shoot at each other. Their fighting and arguments make the Yeki women cry, producing big tears that comes down as rain."

"The thunder's loud noise is very frightening," added Sopunong.

"Don't be afraid of the thunder as it won't hurt you. That's only the Yekis talking angrily. But you can be afraid of their sharp arrows or the lightening. I have seen several trees that have turned brown or black as Yeki's arrow stuck them."

"Tombol, the brother of the chief," continued Pombreol, "was struck as he did not take refuge in a shelter in a storm and Yeki killed him with an arrow of lightening. Don't do anything to annoy Yeki as they may even strike this house down in their anger."

By now the children were all sitting very close to their father with eyes opened wide in fear. He told them that the sooner they respect the Yeki, the better. This is because when a hero dies in a battle his spirit goes to the sky and becomes a Yeki, while a bad man's spirit stays on the ground and becomes an evil spirit.

With that he left the sleepy children with their mothers and walked back to his dwelling place for a good night's rest. Tomorrow it was the time to plan the funeral feast for his late wife.

Eight

CEREMONIAL EXCHANGE

It seemed as if the ancestors were smiling down on Pombreol because everything he did was becoming successful and so he was one of the most admired men of the clan.

Two out of his three wives were pregnant and a young girl from up the stream had been arranged by her father as long as Pombreol was willing to pay five female and seven male pigs with a bamboo of traditional oil for her bride price.

Pombreol knew he could manage that but right now he had something else on his mind. He was giving some wealth to his mother's people called the *'Koar'* to show his appreciation and also so that her spirit in the world of the dead would be happy. He therefore decided that marriage would be later even though a few of the clansmen advised him to pay for the young bride first.

As he gathered more wealth for the *koar* ceremony, he told his two wives to go and ask for some more pigs from their parents, brothers and other extended families. He was also given some wealth by his own friends and

Pombreol

relatives to aid him. When their turn came, he would help according to the amount given to him.

Pombreol and his brother gathered enough pigs, kina shells, bamboo oil and cassowaries to give over to his mother's relatives as a token of appreciation for giving birth to him and raising him to where he is now.

The day before the actual giving, his maternal uncles and cousins were called to see the amount of wealth they were receiving. They arrived with great anticipation and expectation. Every member on the mother's side of the clan was already counting how much wealth they were receiving, according to how much they have given Pombreol and his clan members, and how close they were to each other. As the women lined up their pigs from the biggest to the smallest, the men lined up their kina shells, and the men from the other tribes stood in silence to give their opinions.

The silence was broken by Pombreol as he confidently walked to the middle of the field and greeted everyone. He then announced that he was giving these 24 pigs, two cassowaries, 10 kina shells, two long bamboo oils and one stone axe to appreciate his mum for all the hard work she had done in bringing him into this world and raising him up to be a great warrior.

He then continued to say which person was getting which of the wealth displayed, leaving out a few other things which would be given free. He then told them to come the next day for the final handover. He also told them that the side giving wealth, called the *keond*, will take place as always.

That night, Pombreol could not sleep well. He lay fully awake as the day's event unfolded before him. He could see his elder uncle grinning from ear to ear from pure pride as not every man was able to give wealth to his uncles. Pombreol after all was doing so well he could be declared the chief when the present one dies.

Pombreol moved restlessly on his bed and thought he now owns the title of war lord, but when would he ever become the chief? At that thought he grimaced into the total darkness as he was sure the present chief was still a very vibrant man. As he tossed back and forward on his hard bed, hardly finding any sleep, he recalled his younger uncle's gloomy face in the crowd. He had also left without saying goodbye and this was the real reason why Pombreol was unable to sleep.

His younger uncle was not so happy with the pig he was to be given the next day. In only a few hours' time he would be handing over those things and now he didn't know who to ask to help him with a much bigger pig which he will repay later.

He felt he was almost suffocating as he twisted and turned several times in his sleeping place. All the rest of the men were quietly snoring away after the stressful event. He was still battling with his thoughts when he heard his first wife calling out to him in the pitch of the dark. This really had to be an emergency because ladies were not allowed near the men's house unless whatever it is can't wait. It was already in the middle of the night!

With a heavy heart from the night's ordeal, being careful not to disturb the sleeping men, he walked on his knees towards the entrance of the house to investigate what brought this woman here at an hour like this.

Before his eyes got used to the dark outside, he heard a pig's grunt followed by snuffles, making the low sound seem very loud in the cold air. As he got close enough to see what was happening, he saw his wife standing there with a very huge pig.

No word could come out of his mouth as he realised what had happened. While he was restless on his bed, his wife had walked to her village and asked one of her brothers for a pig to support her husband in the next day's event. He stood still not knowing what to say.

"Because I realised you needed one pig for your younger uncle, I simply went to my brothers and this is what they can afford to give me." She was the one starting the conversation.

Pombreol simply couldn't talk as his throat was so constricted and tears were rolling down his checks. She must not know that I am crying with joy, he thought, as he quickly brushed away the tears with both hands.

The moon was so bright and shadows of nearby trees were dancing in the moonlight. The cold highland's air enveloped his bare body as he stood very still, struggling to say the right words to express himself to his wife for this great act of kindness.

Without thinking, he grabbed the pig by the rope and led his wife to her house. They walked in total silent companionship. His wife fully understood that he had appreciated her so much that he would accompany her to the ladies' dwelling place in the middle of the night.

Pombreol felt a shiver run down his spine and deep down in his groin something else was stirring as he walked his only one true love to her sleeping place. Her last baby had just been weaned off the breast milk so he knew it was just the right time.

As they talked to each other quietly he reached out to hug her close to himself so that she would also feel his desire, when suddenly a shout was heard within the ladies' dwelling place. He pulled his hand right back as if he had just held a red hot stone.

Pombreol

It was his other wife asking why they were talking to each other in the dark.

Pombreol replied, it was none of her business and she should be ashamed of herself for listening in on their private conversation.

"Useless couple talking close to where I sleep," she screamed. Pombreol knew full well that she did not sleep on that side of the house, the very reason why he led his love toward that road. She truly was a pain in the bones.

The first wife demanded to know who the useless wife was. "Sister of a Dog," she shouted back to her. "I have brothers who are men enough to give me wealth anytime to elevate my man up to another level in the society and you, daughter of a good for nothing", she continued. "If I can go in the night and bring a pig this big, you are nothing. All you are capable of is to bear children to my husband, that's who you are".

Pombreol realised these two women's rivalry and argument will go on all through the night and his presence will fuel the argument, so he hugged his wife's hand tightly and walked back to his dwelling place. His desire slowly dying within himself made him want to beat the life out of that intruder.

The fading word he heard from this useless lady was, "tomorrow, you will tell me so you sleep". The argument could go on forever in the night but whoever starts any argument tomorrow will have to pack up and go to her brothers as it was not the time for a heated argument. And he wouldn't mind if it was that woman who is relaxing away in the house arguing with his most beloved wife.

The voices were fading away as he walked into the house and fell on his hard bed on the earth in total exhaustion, falling immediately asleep as his burden of looking for a pig for his unhappy uncle was lifted from his shoulders. Thanks to his one and only true love.

Far in the distance, he could hear the fading melody of courting songs. So, the girls from the village have invited the boys from the other tribe, he thought, and immediately gave a loud snore.

Early the next morning, the whole village was awake with various kinds of noise, as it was going to be an eventful day. Pombreol got up from his sleep and immediately thought of last night's event and again, somewhere in the corner of his brain, was grateful for his wife. He locked it up never to play around with this one woman as she was going to be his strength and support. The others can go if they want to.

As he quickly got up from his sleeping place, Nawe brought him breakfast of sweet potatoes, which he ate as fast as he could for he had a long day ahead. He told his son to collect his tanget leaves and other materials for his decorations. Today the men will dress him up with his warrior body decorations which he had collected and prepared in the days before this event. For sure, today was going to be special for Pombreol. Society will know for sure his potential in being a leader.

Pombreol asked the best body painter to paint and decorate him. His face was painted black with ground up charcoal and special white mud paint in the middle of his face. His kina shell was decorated with red paint and worn around his neck. Being a warrior, he wore his *moka* kina shell as a focal point of his dress. Larger pectoral ornaments made of large mother of pearl, traded for in the downstream trade, had been cut into shape and were displayed on his chest, hanging from a necklace that his head passed through with no difficulty at all.

Pombreol

These kina shells had come a long way and were valuable and scarce. That's why he told the young children not to come near him as he did not want his precious ornament trampled over by children. After all, those shells with two drilled holes at the end where the bindings were to be attached and painted with very scarce red paints were true objects of value. He had repeatedly told his wives and children that this mother of pearl is a sign of wealth and prosperity. Anyone caught near it would be severely dealt with. The family never got near those things in fear of their very lives.

After Pombreol was fully dressed in his entire *moka* gear, he got his bow and arrow and walked to the gathering area where his clan were lining up the wealth to be given to his mother's relatives. Today he walked lightly as he would distribute everything among his mum's clan fairly, including his last uncle who wasn't looking so happy yesterday.

The crowd went silent as the warrior walked proudly into the middle of the field. He purposely chose the higher ground where he could address the crowd. With his bow and arrows gripped tightly in his hands, his decorated body gave him the look of the great warrior that he was.

He counted up all his pigs, kina shells, bamboo oil, and cassowaries and confidently distributed them according to who was getting what. Even the unhappy face from yesterday was smiling happily as he was given the pig brought by his wife in the night. To put more weight on what he was giving, his clansmen gave his maternal relatives some side wealth called the *keond*.

A huge pig was in turn given to Pombreol by the matrilineal clan. He announced straight away that he would kill the exchange pig the next day and share it among those who had helped him making the day's event so successful. A few of the clan's younger boys were selected to prepare for the *mumu* next day. They collected firewood, ferns, leaves and stones.

It was a relief that evening for Pombreol as he felt like a load was removed from his shoulders. Months of raising pigs and weeks of gathering other wealth for this event was not so easy. All he wanted to do was lay down in pure exhaustion, but it was never meant to be. In the men's hut that night, the men talked about how successful the event had been. They were talking to each other and sometimes on top of each others voice in pure pride, as each person gave his best opinion of how successful and popular their clan was becoming.

Pombreol couldn't rest so well with all the noise, so he too got up from his sleeping place and joined the conversation. They talked until their fire slowly burnt out and each man was shivering in the cold of the night.

Pombreol fell asleep with thoughts of how he would share his pork meat the next day running through his mind. After all, his uncles were not losers as they were able to give him this very big pig in return. They deserved all the wealth he had given them and upon that thought, he fell into a deep sleep. He dreamt that his mum was calling him to climb the very high mountain that separates her village with his father's village, and be with his uncle.

He became fully awake after the dream but it was still pitch dark outside. He lay very still as he ran the dream over and over again in his mind. Why should his mum who died a long time ago want him to join her clan, since his duty as a clan warrior lay on his shoulder in his own father's clan?

Pombreol

His mind then flew quickly to his mother, who was always there for him. As a child he would see her in her short grass skirt coming from the gardens with her pigs, with her bag of food from the garden on her head. He smiled to himself in the dark as he recalled how he would roll on the ground and cry his eyes out so mum would put him on her neck on top of the heavy bag. How he would sit there so relaxed, singing all kinds of songs that he heard the men singing in the men's house.

He especially remembered the time when his mum was feeding a very tiny piglet on her bare breast. He was so upset he threw the pig into the open fire, to be immediately burnt up with the open flame. His parents were not happy and belted him so badly; he swore never to do it again. He smiled some more when he recalled the look of fury on his mum's face. He didn't care, as he was comforted again on her breast and this time, both breasts were his to keep; he was never sharing with any piglets. He fell asleep again, badly affected by the dream.

The next day, the people gathered for the party. Pombreol cut up the pork and shared it among his people, giving big pieces to those who helped in his *Koar*.

His two wives started arguing about who should get the pig's intestine that was cleaned and cooked. At first it was just words but after a while of throwing hateful words at each other, both women were rolling on the ground clawing and tearing at each other. The men had quite a time separating them. Upon separation, the first wife said to the other that her brothers were too poor; they gave only two pigs for the compensation payment to their husband's mother's relatives. The other replied that the first one's brothers were too lazy to look after pigs and gave three small ones with hairs like her very own pubic hair.

Pombreol

As they continued their verbal attack, calling names at each other, Pombreol told them to stop - to which nobody paid any attention. He was so angry he grabbed the juicy cooked intestine and threw it in the nearby river, which carried it away. The argument stopped immediately as it was a common knowledge that when Pombreol was angry, he beat his wives without mercy. Everyone went silent.

He walked off to the men's house without turning back. The ladies started lowering their voices, still angry with each other, but no one dared to speak up for fear of being beaten up by Pombreol.

The next day he was told wild pigs had destroyed the taro garden. He got his two sons and made off to the garden to fix the fence where the pigs had made their way in. Because they couldn't wait for breakfast, they all carried some raw *kaukau* to roast and eat in the garden as they worked.

Walking ahead with his boys right behind him, Pombreol was an angry man. He couldn't imagine his precious taro garden being destroyed by pigs. If the pigs were wild, nothing could be done about it but if someone owned that pig... he gripped his stone axe tightly upon that thought.

The two sons knew what it meant when their father was quiet and so they too followed quietly. They knew someone was in for a very big problem as they watched their father's shoulder muscles bulge suddenly as he gripped his axe tightly. It was like that all the way to the garden.

The sons could understand their father because recently the villagers talked a lot like they never had before about that taro garden. Several times they had heard their father talking proudly about how he would

Pombreol

share the taro. And now this; it really wasn't good news to bear. Precious wealth or not, one pig was really in for big trouble as people need food to stay alive, not wealth. As the two boys discussed these issues, they could see their father reaching the top of the hill and disappearing round a twisted corner of the road.

Upon reaching the garden they gave a loud cry of joy. They found that the destruction was only near the fence where a wild pig broke in. The pig apparently realized that it wasn't a *kaukau* garden, for taros are usually bitter to taste, therefore it left without digging more.

After fixing the fence, they all weeded the garden and did other minor things that needed mending. They worked hard the whole day. Then they gathered their few things and a dry piece of wood each for firewood, and walked home.

On his way home Pombreol thought of nothing but a hearty dinner with left over pork from yesterday's feast. Upon reaching the village he merely nodded at people who greeted him and went straight to his wives' house. He rarely did that and his wives knew he went to their house when he was very, very hungry.

When he reached the destination he asked his first wife for his food. "Go and get it from your other wife," was the reply. When he asked the second, she didn't even talk.

So these two ladies hadn't recovered from the previous day's problem. Well, that was their problem and right then Pombreol was so hungry that his anger was at its boiling point. Walking out with pure fury he went straight for his bow and arrow and ordered the two ladies to come out of their house.

Pombreol

Realizing their grave mistake, the two ladies came out. He ordered them to a nearby tree and called his sons to bring the strongest bush vines he had left to tie his bananas. The boys brought them willingly as they, too, were very hungry - those few *kaukaus* eaten in the garden weren't enough to fill the men's tummy.

"Looks like your fathers never told you that a hungry man is an angry man. I'll show you and you will never forget." He tied the two ladies to the same tree back to back and belted the hell out of them.

"Now you know who the boss is around here. I'll leave you two here till tomorrow so every woman who hears of this will take their proper place in the society and obey their husband's every command. After all, we paid for you with no less wealth," he yelled. The men who were there agreed to all his words and even added some of their own thoughts. But the women folk ran to their houses in fear and shame. Few of them had ever seen anything like that.

Heranong, his daughter after Nawe, brought out several small *kaukaus* she had cooked for herself, giving them to her father, who got them and threw back at her.

"Lazy girl, who is going to eat all this small *kaukau*? Am I your pig? One day I will really teach you a good lesson so you don't do the same thing to your husband and bring a bad name to me." Heranong didn't even hear part of her father's words for she had run for her own dear life.

Being fully satisfied with all the talks, Pombreol strolled back to the men's house for his tobacco pipe and stayed smoking into the night with his men while his wives slept outside, still tied to the tree. Nobody dared untie the two frightened ladies for fear of Pombreol's arrow.

Pombreol

Straight after midnight, when he was sure his father was snoring away with other men, Nawe quietly got up from his side and walked out, prepared to say he was going to the toilet if someone asked. But nobody did. He was sure they were all gone to another land, wherever that may be.

When he had laid down earlier, pretending to be fast asleep, he had made up his mind to help his mothers, for he didn't want those spirits that travelled in the night to take his mothers away. After all, they were his mothers and he was sorry for them. He didn't let his brother know because he might tell their father. One can never know what his father might do to him for planning such a thing against him.

As he walked silently towards the tree he knew that his father's fury would be poured down on him like a hail storm, but his desire to help his mothers overpowered his fear. However, to be on the safe side, he had already made up his mind to go to his mother's village to stay until his father cooled off. Somewhere in the corner of his mind he knew his father would send for him as he wouldn't allow his favourite son to be sleeping with other people for a long time.

Upon reaching his mothers, he realised they were both very cold and stiff, making them unable to talk. He immediately started cutting the vines, as he had planned earlier, with the sharpened piece of bamboo he had brought from the men's house. He couldn't afford to waste any time as his father or anybody spying on him might find out what he was doing and report him to his father - who might come down very hard on him.

As soon as he had released the two women, he led them to their house. They were weak from the beating earlier and cold. Nawe made a huge fire for them. After, they gained their strength and were able to talk; he cautioned them to talk quietly and gave them some food and water to drink.

Early in the morning, after overnighting in the ladies house, Nawe gathered his few belongings that he had pre-packed before the rescue operation, and took off with his mother to her village. The other lady also went to her parents too.

When Pombreol found out what had happened he was actually proud of his son for being brave, and sent for his son to come back at once. He also took a kina shell each to his two wives' brothers as a payment for his cruel treatment to his wives and brought them all back to his village.

Nine

BETRAYAL OF CLANSMEN & CONSEQUENCES

*I*n the men's hut that night, the men talked about how successful the event was. They talked to each other, sometimes on top of each other, in pure pride as each person gave his best opinion.

Their discussion moved onto something serious - Pombreol's clansmen Wenpiol and his brother, who had lost all their children to some kind of sickness that hadn't responded to the treatment of the village spirit medium and witch doctor. The latest one died most recently because the infant's head swelled up within months of birth, which showed that their father had betrayed one of his own clansmen, causing his death. Now the clan's god was about to wipe the whole family out. Not only did they lose their children but, as far as Pombreol could remember, their grandfather and their father had died young too.

The village chief explained to the two brothers that the infant's swollen head could only mean that their father's brain was filled with water instead of normal brain, resulting from betrayal of his very own clansman, one's true brother. Pombreol further announced that the truth established from secret, sacred messages and teaching handed down by their ancestors must be retold among them, so that proper interpretation is done. After that, the witch doctor would be hired to bring total healing to the clan.

Wenipiol and his brother Paiki had no idea. The oldest men in the clan were made to talk. So the oldest man began his story.

"Once upon a time, in this great land, there lived a very rebellious man named Luwi. He was a man who had no conscience at all. He would steal from people's gardens and houses, and terrorised weak women and helpless young girls. Unfortunately, he was the only brother of the father of Wenpiol and Paiki. To compensate for all the problems that Luwi was creating, his brother's (Wenpiol's Dad) precious wealth was given out and a deep hatred was developed for his younger brother.

"Day after day, he was advised of his social obligation and other ethical issues of living on this land but he never took any advice. He surely was thought to have been controlled by the devil himself. Until one final time, when Luwi was said to have raped a young woman, her relatives rampaged his house and stole his very large pig. Luwi had no proper house, garden or wealth so all the burdens of his bad activities were laid on the shoulder of Paiki his brother. His wife had run away with their only son for fear of her own dear life.

"This time, he could not control his fury. Therefore he arranged for his brother Luwi to be killed and thrown into the mighty Lai River. People were only too glad to terminate him as long as his blood brother gave the secret order, as everyone felt the effect of his existence on the land. As he was cornered to be killed, he uttered the following final words, 'because I have been causing problems in this land, you are killing me but if my immediate clan men are involved in this, I will turn into a mosquito and look after our drinking creeks, our mushrooms and our whole land.'

"They cracked his skull and smashed his brains without mercy or second thoughts. His dead body was finally thrown into the mighty Lai River, which washed his poor body downstream. Of course, the whole tribe did not know of the event that had taken place, but nobody missed him either. He was one of the most hated and loneliest men who have ever lived.

"However, his soul has not found a place to dwell and is still wandering around in the bush, restless and crying in distress in the land. Several people have already met his spirit that had turned into a ghost. And his final words were a curse. Those very words meant that his spirit had turned into a dangerous kind of spirit called the 'Su Tomo'. This kind of spirit will visit down to the third generation of Wenpiol and his brother's family. The entire male population in that family will be killed and be wiped out by this powerful spirit and nobody will be capable enough to stop it.

"If they wanted to escape from that, they would not have been involved at all in his killing. However, since he was involved, he should have left for his mother's or wives' village so he didn't eat from the same land. Because he did not flee to his mother's land on that same day of the killing and had eaten food found on this same land where his brother's blood had fallen, he and his family cannot escape from the curse."

The old man finished his narrative by adding that all males in that family would still die if nothing significant was done quickly. It was against the teaching of the ancestors for a brother to kill his blood brother or plan for his brother to be killed. If such things have happened, and his blood has been poured on the soil that you both own together, you and your sons will be sick from eating from the same land.

The old man then concluded that what they were seeing today in the family of Wenpiol and his brother was the result of what their grandfather did; therefore, they needed to call the spirit medium to fix the mess and save the lives of the entire male line in the family of Wenpiol and his brother.

At that point, the village chief told Wenpiol and his brother to provide a pig which will be slaughtered and its spleen will be prepared in spices and cooked. This will then be cut up and eaten, shared among the sons of Wenpiol and his brothers' sons.

All the men present in the men's dwelling house were all taken aback by this story. Without much to talk about, Wenpiol and his brother were to provide the pig tomorrow and the medium would cast his spell over the pig and do his other bits to keep the spirit away from the family and causing more deaths.

For this ritual to work well, the son of the dead man Luwi, who was taken away by his mum, was called in. In unity and oneness, the pig was provided the next day and its spleen *(hepkuso)* was specially cooked. It was then shared among Wenpiol's sons and his brother and the son of Luwi, in front of the spirit medium who was chanting away in unfamiliar language the whole time. The rest of the pork was shared among the rest of the clan and feasted on, especially by the men and young boys of the clan.

A few live pigs and other wealth were given by Wenpiol to the one son who was left behind, as a compensation payment and to say sorry on behalf of those who were involved but are now in the world of the Dead. The magician then declared that these would solve the issues of all sons in the family of Wenpiol and his brother from dying young. Having heard that, all the men and boys of the clan walked back to their sleeping place in a happier mood.

Ten

MARRIAGE

When there was a young man ready for marriage, Pombreol and his whole clan always gathered together and discussed the matter. This time it was Sap who was the focus of the discussion. Pombreol and his men decided that Sap, who had just returned from his final initiation, needed a wife.

Sap sat among them but he had no say for this was an important decision which was to be made by his clan's elders. It was always the way of the people of this land that choices of marriage partners were rarely left to the individual. As always, after his initiation into adult society, he had courted several girls under close supervision from the elders, but the final selection would come from the village elders.

As he sat and listened, he knew that out of the several girls he was courting, it was only Sorwanong, the girl from downstream, that he loved. But if they selected someone else, he could always settle for the second best. There never was any choice left to him or any other boys of the village when it came to selecting brides for them.

Pombreol

As the discussion continued, he heard someone saying, "The young girl who brought the pig's belly is the one we are buying."

"No, we are going for the one who brought the bag of yams. She is hard working and has lots of exchange pigs to bring to us," said another.

Nobody mentioned anything about the one who brought the taros and it saddened Sap, but what could he do. He had told her already that he really loved her. But if his clansmen went for someone else he did not have much choice. And she had said that if they did go for someone else that she would never marry a man in her whole life. That was their promise to each other on their final courting night. He will always remember those words with her, probably their last.

The discussion went on and on for a while until they settled for the daughter of the chief in the next village. "She is going to cost us more," someone warned from the back.

"We are not exactly poor. We can show them that we are somebody, too," someone else answered.

The next morning, Sap's father and his mother's elder brother, as was the custom, went to ask the father of the girl if he was willing to give his daughter to their son in marriage. The chief of the village agreed to give away his daughter because Pombreol's clan had great warriors and they had never lost any tribal wars.

Back home Sap was sad because they had decided on a different girl rather than Sorwanong. After all, she was the daughter of the chief and he indeed had no choice. The owners of the wealth for the bride price had made their choice. Since he had no choice he should just prepare himself to be the chief's son in law. At the end of the day, what man wouldn't want to be a chief's son in law?

He did feel lucky as not every boy gets a chief's daughter as a bride. As for his love for Sorwanong, if the gods were on his side, he would accumulate enough wealth and could always have her for his second wife. After all, he was the most wanted boy in the village. Everyone thought he was so handsome and everywhere he went girls were always fighting for him.

When the chief told his daughter about the marriage, she got her best grass skirt and wore it, and her special bag made especially for a bride. She took her best friend and one of her uncle's wives to Sap's village with the two men who came for her.

The girl's relatives were told to come and see the bride price after five days. As the group reached the village, everybody gathered around to see the newcomers, especially the bride. There was excitement in the air but Sap wasn't around. He was too shy to come near her. After all, he had never once courted her and he did not know how to properly meet a girl who he had never courted and yet was now to be his wife.

The newcomers had been given a house to stay in and food provided for them. The bride was then asked to provide her bridal net bag so that kina shells could be arranged by village elders for her to carry around until the payment of the bride price. This was the first ceremony of the bride price payment process.

The bride and her ladies stayed in the groom's village for five days while relatives of the groom from far and near gathered pigs, kina shells, cassowaries, traditional salt and oil for the bride price. During their stay the young bride and her ladies sang special traditional wedding songs which were meant to trigger people to bring more valuable gifts. Upon hearing the heart-touching wedding songs, the old women wept with bitter-sweet memories as they remembered their golden days. Relatives from near and far brought in wealth for the payment of the bride.

After the given days were over, the relatives arrived to see the bride price and to decide if it was worthy of her. After adding everything up they wanted three more big pigs. If the three pigs were not added they would take the girl back to their village. The discussions and the exchange of words went on and on until four more pigs instead of three were added to the collection, so the bride's father didn't have to think that the groom and his clansmen were poor.

The next day, Pombreol and his clansmen went to the bride's village with all their bride price items to be given away to her relatives. They were then given several pigs in exchange, which they brought to their village for the wedding feast.

Before they settled in for the night, a few of the elders of the village performed the second part of the wedding ceremony for new bride called the *'Tind Weh Nu'*. The new young bride was asked to bring her specially made smaller net bag in which small bundles of red and yellow paint used for decorating one's face were placed. These small bundles were placed among magic leaves called the *'esh weh nu'*. These were small red leaves from a thick bush and were only kept by the magic men of the village. These magic leaves were used to separate every bundle of paint *'tind weh'* placed inside the bride's smaller net bag. The bag, now called a *'tind weh* and *esh weh nu'*, was placed carefully inside a bigger net bag especially made for a new bride called *'nu hepi'*. After carefully arranging them, this bag was placed on the head of the bride. The village chief then asked her to take care of the bag with its special contents. After the whole marriage ceremony was over, the bag's contents were to be returned to the chief himself.

During her initiation period when she was entering adulthood, the village women elders had already taught her and the other girls her age about this ceremony, so she was aware of the rules for the *'Tind Weh* and *Esh Weh Nu'*.

At that time she and other girls in the group would giggle a lot despite the stern, hard faces of the old ladies. The thought of marriage and going through all these ceremonies felt like some silly joke. In those times she would dream away and imagine some young and handsome warriors fighting for her, but never once dreamt of this groom. Now she was thankful to those ladies for the teaching.

At that thought she suddenly looked around and, there in the crowd, he was staring back at her, causing her face to become red and hot. With sudden warmth of her body, she looked away and hoped that nobody saw that exchange of secret looks between the husband and wife-to-be. At first glance she could see how handsome he looked and wondered why she didn't want to marry him in the first place, but was forced to by her father. She was now thankful to her father for selecting one of the most handsome men in the land to be her husband.

All of a sudden she shivered and her mind floated back to the present ceremony. The magic man was now carefully placing her bag with the special contents on her head, reminding her of the rules that she had to follow as a new bride with this bag on her head.

Pombreol

That night the young bride left her *'tind weh* and *esh weh nu'* in the doorway because the house was smoky. In the days that followed, the village women looked for young sweet potatoes in new gardens only and fed the bride, as she had the special bag containing the precious cargo.

Cassowaries were rare and highly valued and used in payment of bride price as well as other ceremonial activities.

Very early in the morning following the bride price payment, elderly ladies from the village woke the new bride to perform the ceremony called the *'so mo tilal pismi'*. Paplin, the new bride, was aware she would be awoken by this group of ladies. Before anybody else was awake they led her to the top of the hill where the ceremony will take place.

She quietly followed them to the top of the hill overlooking the valley. In a whisper, she was asked by the chief's wife to keep still and watch the magic lady raise the morning birds from their sleep. As she stared into the dark, the magic woman was chanting words into the open air, looking in all directions. To her great amazement, a sleepy bird was heard in the southern direction, which meant someone from the south was bringing wealth for her next lot of bride price.

By now beautiful lights had spread across the valley and had chased the darkness away. The elders led their bride down the hill towards the village, smiling happily, as their trip was not wasted. A bird had sung indeed, therefore someone was bringing some wealth from the direction of the bird as a contribution to the ongoing payment of bride price.

In the evening, a huge pig was brought by Sap's grandfather who was from the southern part of the

Pombreol

valley. The women of the village were all excited as their magic had won.

Two days had gone by and on the morning of the third day she was still lying down with her friend when she heard her father-in-law calling her. "Paplin, you have to get up so we can go and cover your footprint with this pig." She got up quickly and got into her traditional bridal cloth.

This was the second part of the bride price ceremony called the '*ank koes*'. They took the pig to her village, gave it to an uncle, who was still complaining that he only got a small pig. He in return gave her a kina shell which she took back to her groom's relatives.

Leaving her uncle's wife behind, the new bride took her best friend, who was a young girl. She would be living with Sap's parents until the third lot of bride price was paid. Then she would be ready to go to live in the groom's new house. Back in the village she and her friend stayed close together, following the advice given by her village women.

Five days had gone and now the final and most important part of the marriage ceremony was to take place. This was the final giving called the '*ki top*' and '*sumbo tenk*', when the groom and the bride would go alone to give some wealth to the parents only. After this final bride price payment ceremony, the bride's parents would never call Sap's name and the bride's mother would always have her head covered in his presence.

Sap's father, who was wealthy enough, gave two big pigs and a lump of salt to the young couple to take to the parents. "Paplin, this should really satisfy your parents, and when you return this afternoon you should be ready to remove your bridal clothes and live with your husband in his new house." With a slight shiver she prepared for her final trip to her village as a bride.

As the couple travelled together neither made an attempt to start any conversation. They both were too shy as they had never been alone together. After travelling in an uncomfortable silence for a while, the pig that she was holding started pulling her into the bush. She pulled and pulled but in vain. Obviously she needed some help but Sap didn't know what to do. As Sap stood transfixed and watched, Paplin knew he wanted to help but she couldn't allow that. She had to somehow show him that she could handle the pig. After all, taming a pig was a woman's job.

If she couldn't handle this he might get all his bride price back and marry another woman, which she couldn't stand since he was such a good looking man. As if the pig had read her thoughts, it found its way back and they continued silently again, each with different thoughts.

Arriving at the village, they handed what they had brought to the parents. The mother was not satisfied with the pig they took for her and said so. But the father told her to shut up and sent the girl home quickly, for rain clouds were already gathering. A father's words were always a rule in that area so Paplin gathered her things and left with her husband. This time Sap took his young bride to the new house he built as part of his initiation ceremony. Having paid all of the bride price, he was now a proud husband.

Next full moon they would have a big feast with all the exchanged pigs, except the one female pig which would be left behind to have piglets as a start of wealth for the new family. If the gods were on his side by twelve full moons he should have enough pigs, and maybe a son...

Thinking about a son, he suddenly started shivering. Therefore, he turned to his house and thought of how he was going to approach his bride for the first time. He just wished someone would have told him properly about that. What he knew were just vague stories from boys who didn't have much experience on lying with a new bride. Anyway, no sweat. His fathers had managed, so somehow he would too.

That night Sap went to sleep early but sleep wouldn't come. He lay awake pretending to be asleep. He wasn't even sure if Paplin was sleeping peacefully. The next day he would make sure he talked to her and try to make both of them comfortable. Tonight was only the first night. He'd leave it at that.

The next day they both got up earlier than usual and were making a fire for their breakfast when Paplin's younger brother arrived.

"Mother isn't satisfied with the pig yesterday and she sent me to bring you back," he said, between heavy breaths. Even though Sap argued that a pig and lump of salt were enough, the boy couldn't go back without her. So Paplin and her brother went back to their village.

It was another restless night for Sap as his father had no more pigs to bring Paplin back. As he woke up the next morning, there was someone at the door. It was Pombreol. He had brought Sap one very big female pig.

"Go give it to your mother-in-law. That will close her mouth forever," he said. It was well known that unsatisfied mothers who took their daughters away were asking for female pigs.

Sap could not think of any words to express his happiness but only nodded at what this great warrior and upcoming wealthiest man was saying. Sap then took the pig to Paplin's mum, who readily accepted it with a silly grin, and he brought his bride back home again.

That night he couldn't keep far away from Paplin for fear that they might come for her again. He only hoped that she would have a boy if it was possible from this somewhat very uncomfortable first union.

After a few struggles he had managed it, despite several painful attempts on both Paplin and himself. He felt like he was a real man and could hardly wait for the next time. For now he would wait patiently as he saw that Paplin was looking very uncomfortable the next morning, always looking in another direction when he looked at her. Anyway, for the kind of experience last night, he could wait a lifetime for this woman to want to have a go at it again.

Even if she was always looking away, it did not affect Sap so much. It would be impossible for her to run away as the final bride price was paid. Therefore she was his to do whatever he wanted. With a smile that lit up his handsome face, he planned carefully in his mind how he would approach her again in the night.

Eleven

SACRIFICES TO THE SPIRITS

For three full moons there hadn't been any rain at all. People of this part of the land were unable to plough their land or plant any crops at all as the land had all dried up and was too dry to do any farming at all. All their carefully stored seedlings were already becoming too old. Everywhere Pombreol went, people were complaining, for within a few months their seedlings would be useless and there would be great hunger in the land.

All the drinking creeks had dried up and springs of life-giving water had all disappeared. Children had to look for drinking water from much bigger flowing rivers which were already getting smaller by the passing days. If the dry spell continued then there would be no water anywhere in the land. The ground was cracking everywhere and the soil was too hot to plant anything. In the nights, from what used to be cool nights, it was getting colder and colder and the people did not know what to do. In the morning and during the day, the sky was cloudless with an everlasting blue colour. A fine blue fog covered the blue mountains, showing rain was far, far away.

Pombreol lay restless in his resting place. Tonight was so cold, like no other nights. Even the hard earth, which had most of the time provided comfort and warmth for him, was now very cruel, for the cold was unbearable and uncomfortable.

He was sure sleep was far away as more pressing burdens crept up into his mind and added to his insomnia. One of those pressing issues was the fact that there was going to be a famine in the land and he did not know what he would do to feed his family.

As he twisted and turned on his sleeping place, he felt so cold he was sure he would die if he didn't get up to make the fire. Pombreol raked up the dying embers, added a few dry twigs, and soon had the fire crackling up cheerily, giving him that much desired warmth.

Silently the rest of the occupants crawled around the fire place that Pombreol had built. It was now glowing brightly, releasing heat into the cold atmosphere so that the bare skinned men relaxed in its comforting warmth, making them feel sleepy. As Pombreol and his men sat around the fireplace, they all decided that it was the coldest night and that something ought to be done about it.

Early the next morning, the whole village came alive when a call went around for everyone to gather at the gathering place for an emergency meeting. When everyone had gathered, the village chief stood up from his position and addressed his people.

"My good people, I do not know what we have done to offend the goddess of rain, but if this dry season continues, we are all doomed to death. Therefore we have to do something about this situation. Maybe we didn't offer enough the last offering time, or those gods are still not satisfied and they want us to offer another lot of sacrifices soon. Maybe, that's why they are withholding the rain. Who knows the mind of the gods? All I know is that we need to make some more sacrifices and offerings soon."

The whole clan decided that the offerings would start as a family unit, then clan sacrifices would come after the family sacrifices. As soon as the chief was finished, one overly confident young man wanted to know how many more pigs the gods wanted because they had done the last offering not long ago.

"Hey, be careful what you say or he will bring more suffering on us and this time we will make you responsible for our sufferings. Do you want to find out?" someone yelled from the back.

"I am sorry," said a much less confident young man now, and sat down.

After much discussion, the chief told each family to kill a big pig with no blemish or disease as a family sacrifice. This must happen the next day. Perhaps the drought was because some people sacrificed diseased and small pigs in their last offering. Everyone agreed to those decisions and went on their way to prepare for the family sacrifice. Pombreol and his family selected one of their very healthy male pigs and prepared all the things needed for this sacrifice.

Early next day smoke was seen rising from every family sacrificial house. The sacrifice called the *'Maip Tomo'* was going on. The *'Maip Tomo'* was a sacrifice done in the small separate houses built by every family for their family sacrifices.

Pombreol

Pombreol told his sons during the process that this sacrifice was given to the ancestor's spirits so they would not be angry with his family and withhold the rain. He told them that this sacrifice will also prompt the ancestors to provide protection, safety and guidance for his family during this dry season.

Despite the *Maip Tomo* sacrifices, days had passed with not a cloud in the sky. The dry spell continued with its damage to food gardens. Pombreol sadly told his family that if this type of dry season continued, they should all prepare to go and be with their ancestors. With his shoulders drooping down, he sadly walked to the men's house.

That night was the coldest night of all nights. In the men's house Pombreol got up several times to keep the fire going. The next morning people found their food gardens had being destroyed by frost. So the *'pipi'* had come to damage their food gardens for the second time.

This time the people were very sure the goddess who lives in the sacred house, the *'Kevil da'*, was surely not happy and was out to destroy them. This resulted in bringing the sacrificial offering time closer. Words were then sent to other tribes throughout the area to prepare a big offering ceremony to the goddess of rain.

Because this dry spell had gone beyond its normal season, other tribesmen agreed to do what Pombreol and his tribesmen were planning, and started the preparation straight away. It was planned and agreed that by next full moon the sacrificial ceremony called the *'Kevil da'* would take place. This sacrifice would not involve the women folk. The women knew it was a men's offering so they went about with their other activities leaving the men with their secretive preparation.

Meanwhile the people called the messenger of the goddess, called the 'rat man', who lives alone in the forest, to consult the goddess and find out whether she was angry and if she would accept the offering. The rat man gathered all the people and brought out a dead rat from his bag. He then laid it on the ground and told the people to look at it closely to make sure it was really dead.

When they were satisfied it was dead, he got some leaves and wrapped the rat and tied it up with strong bush vines. He then picked up the bundle and rubbed it between his two hands while chanting in some strange language. After chanting and rubbing for a long time, he unwrapped the bundle and to everyone's surprise the rat was gone!

As everyone stood silently, the rat man was heard announcing that the goddess was ready for their offering because the dead rat has disappeared into thin air. Upon this announcement, all walked slowly back home as this offering involved the men only. Any details of the sacrifices were always kept secret from the women.

At Pombreol's village, preparation was underway. Very early in the morning the sacrificial leaders were heard shouting to ask all women to stay in their house while the sacrifice preparation was underway. For his family, Pombreol selected his first wife's biggest pig, which he took to the sacrificial place without notifying her. The other men and young boys brought in their contribution as well.

Young boys were then sent to the bush to collect materials to decorate the men's bodies. Thick black charcoal was collected, smashed up and left in long containers in traditional oil. Darker tanket plant leaves were collected and left in small creeks to keep fresh. Large

Pombreol

bamboo containers were also prepared for collection of blood for the offering.

In the morning of the offering day, Pombreol and his men got up very early and slaughtered the selected pigs. All the blood was carefully collected in the long bamboo containers. When the container was filled, a piece of wood was used as a protective seal for the opening and more bamboo was filled and prepared.

Men from each family were decorated according to the number of containers of blood. They were all painted heavily with the previously prepared charcoal from head to toe. The black tanget leaves were used to cover their buttocks while their front was covered with a traditionally woven piece of cloth. Then each decorated man was made to stand in front of another with a container of blood on his shoulder. Each man was told by the rat man to look to his right, never looking in front, back or the left. The men were made to stand very close to each other.

Pombreol felt the weight of the container on his bare shoulder getting heavier but stood very quietly. When he felt the man in front of him starting to move, he also took every step that this man took. In this way, he was sure no single movement was seen by an observer from a distance.

Those who were watching were never allowed to talk or make any noise. All the younger boys were left in their houses with their mothers and the girls during this ceremony, so the rest of the males watched in total silence. Not even the slightest movement was detected as the row of men silently carried out their ceremony. The ceremony took quite a time.

Pombreol

As the men got near the sacred house, where the goddess overnighted on her way to her final destination, each man poured his container of blood around the house and then inside the house, also rubbing some of that blood on a small rock kept inside. Inside the ceremonial hut, Pombreol and a few men from other clans who were chosen to go inside the house, were told by the controller of the ceremony not to look up or around them. They were to look down only, until the controller said the word *'saina sharrp'*. Then they would look towards the mountain called Saina in that village where the sacrifice was going on.

As Pombreol looked down he became aware that the ceremonial house they were in was built in such a way that not even the slightest hole was to be found in it, but he felt comfortable among the men chosen from the surrounding tribes.

Then the most anticipated moment came, the controller said aloud the word they were all listening for, *'saina sharrp'*. Immediately Pombreol looked towards the direction of the tallest mountain in the area and for a brief moment saw strange people with long smooth hair floating by. Then nothing happened.

After that somewhat short vision inside the ceremonial house, all were sent back to their respective villages. Pombreol wondered how this great number of men were able to fit inside that small sacrificial house, and further wondered if all of them saw what he saw. He was not able to ask as talking was forbidden in the area, but for sure he will ask one of his tribesmen who also was selected to be with him in the ceremony. Pombreol then went to search for his tribesmen to walk home to their village for the big feast with the left over pork that awaited them.

And feasting was what the men folk did. As for the ladies, they stayed indoors awaiting the call from the *timb* leaders allowing them to come out of their houses.

Because there was still more than enough, Pombreol gathered all the fat pieces from the pork and hid them under a flat stone in the creek for future use. Smaller bundles were left on top of banana trees around the men's house so they could eat them after a few days. When the feasting was done, the leader sent messages to the ladies that the ceremony was over and they were now released to carry out their daily activities.

Days later, thick clouds gathered in the otherwise clear blue sky but no rain fell except for several days of a few drops in the night along with flashes of lightning and thunder like never heard before. Kids ran for the comfort of their mothers who gathered them in their arms, while the men huddled together in the men's house as it continued.

Then there were a few more drops. Then suddenly the long awaited rain poured down and everyone talked excitedly to each other. The gods had now accepted their offering. Very excited naked kids played in the rain like never before. Even some adults joined in the excitement. Their wish for the rain to continue in the night came true as large drops of rain were heard splitting the leaves of the banana trees around their house. The rivers and creeks were slowly swelling up, they were sure.

As buckets and buckets of rain continued to pour the next morning, talk in each village was all about how good their offerings had been for the goddess to send rain that fast. Pombreol could remember the last sacrifice which had not been accepted too well since rain was not sent soon enough, and he mentioned that in the heated discussions among the men who were now staying indoors due to so much rain.

As days passed, it kept on pouring down like never before. It seemed as though the sky had burst open and was refusing to close. This of course wasn't good because how could people plant in weather as bad as this? Why was the goddess sending too much rain? Was it because they had offered too much? Such were the questions everybody had in their mind.

Pombreol thought it was because they had offered too much. Other times pigs offered were from each clan. But this time a pig came from each family which would be more. Who knew the minds of the gods? On the other hand, this could be happening because some people had smartly talked against the gods before the sacrifices. Whatever the reason was, everyone was sure that another sacrifice should be done so the goddess sends enough rain, but not too much. This rain was almost killing them.

This time they planned on doing the *'Timb Da'*. The *timb warsumbo*, or the leaders, whistled at each other announcing the *'sol timb'* during the day. Upon hearing this whistle all the women ran as fast as they could to their house to hide, for this whistle was yet announcing another sacrifice.

Little Parin had followed her mum to the garden, finding shelter from the forever pouring rain under their special umbrella made from pandanus leaves. As she followed her mum back in a hurry, being pulled in all directions as her little umbrella got stuck in twigs and other branches along the pathway, she was so frustrated, she was surely asking her mummy, what this was all about?

Upon reaching the warm shelter of their home, Parin asked her mum why she raced back to the house as if the devil himself was after her very own life.

"Daughter, the whistle we heard was signaling for us women to leave what we were doing and run straight to our houses to hide ourselves because the men will be doing their men only ceremonial offering to the gods, called the *sol timb da*."

"Why do the ladies have to hide?" asked Parin, sitting very close to the fireplace to get her bare, wet, cold body warm quickly.

"Because if we ladies see the face of any men during this sacrificial period, we will surely die. The sacrifice will take two days to finish. After the sacrifice is over, we ladies will be called to take part in the final process which is the big dance and singsing. We will only go out of the house to use the toilet. During that time, if you meet a man, cover yourself with your net bag or the local umbrella so you don't see their face and die instantly."

Parin was too scared to die too soon, therefore she decided that she was not going outside to use any toilet for the next two days. However, she wanted to know why there was yet another sacrificial ceremony when they just had one.

"It's because the goddess of rain has sent too much rain now. We won't be able to plough our land and plant our already overdue seeds from the dry spell as our lands are now full of water everywhere. Not only is there pools of water everywhere but there is also as much mud due to the continuous rain," her mother replied.

"Who is this goddess who seems to be so powerful?" Parin wanted to know.

This time her mum made herself comfortable around the fireplace and began her story on how the goddess passed through their village. Her tone of voice changed as she started her narrative.

"Once upon a time in a village far in the east there lived 10 young girls. One of them was an albino while the rest were brown skinned. They had never seen a male human in their life.

"Among them the albino was so active and strong. They raised a lot of pigs but never ate them. As soon as a pig had died, they would weep bitterly over it and bury it as if they were burying a human being.

"This had gone on for a while until one fine day, something happened. One very handsome man called Sundo Owl arrived in this village. As he approached, he sat on a hill overlooking the village when he heard wailing and cries of distress in the village below him.

"As the funeral possession approached a cemetery close to where he was sitting, he saw the corpse being laid down to rest, as the weeping got louder and louder. Hiding himself well behind the bush, he watched the ten very beautiful girls painfully going on about their burial.

"To his uttermost surprise, he saw that the corpse was a dead pig. He could not believe that ten young girls should be so affected by the death of a pig, therefore he approached them.

"When the girls saw him approaching, they were so terrified they ran in all directions. He then unearthed the dead pig, took it straight to their house, butchered it and cooked it.

"While he was cooking, the girls out of curiosity walked back to their house but watched him silently, on the alert to run away if they saw any danger from this total stranger. However, he went about smoothly in what he was doing. Sensing no danger at all, they walked into their house one by one and sat close together at one corner.

"Sundo Owil carefully offered them some of the cooked pieces of pork, indicating that it was safe to eat what they thought was a human being that had been buried for a long time. As they reluctantly accepted the offer and tasted it, they liked it and took part in the meal. The stranger then realised that, the ladies had neither anal or vaginal openings; therefore he sharpened a few pieces of bamboo and planted them on the banana trees in front of their house.

"The young girls after eating wanted to empty their bladder as well as their rectum but due to no orifices they could not get rid of them. In their struggle and distress, they rubbed themselves on the banana trees which had sharp pieces of bamboo planted upon them. The sharp bamboos opened up their bodies so that they had anal and vaginal openings.

"Meanwhile the albino young girl, in total confusion, ran up and down inside the house looking for a way to escape for the main door had already been shut by Sundo Owil when all the girls entered the house. As she desperately looked for her escape route, she found a very tiny hole in the wall of the house. She escaped through that hole never to return to their house again."

Pombreol's wife realised it was getting dark outside and the fire had gone out. She stopped her story and gathered more firewood to add onto the fireplace. After the fire picked up its warmth and light again, the children, who by now had grown in number and were sitting very quietly, begged their mother to continue.

"Where did she go?" asked someone among the little group.

"She walked towards the direction of the sunset," came the reply.

"Well then, continue the story," said the small boy who was sitting very close to the narrator.

"She walked and walked, only resting when it was dark.

Where she rested, men from that area built a small hut for her shelter. Different names were given to those shelters. In one village, they called it 'Wendeya Da', 'Hepya Da' in another village and in our village they called it the 'Plem Da'.

"The last village that she rested before she went over the mountain to her final resting place is called the 'Kema Kumb Saiel'.

"Ever since she passed through, men have been bringing sacrifices to her. Once in a while, men climb the tall mountains on the western end of this valley to bring sacrifices to her final resting place, somewhere in a cave.

"The last sacrifices the men of this land took to her hut, called the 'Plem Da'. But instead of just enough rain, the sky had opened its mouth and rain has been pouring down like never before. That's why the men are whistling at each for another sacrifice so that the goddess gives just enough rain.

"Every time sacrifices are made to this albino woman, only men are involved in this ceremony until we are invited into the final process called the 'Timb Ole' which is the end process of the Timb. That's why we ladies have to stay indoors."

After two days the ladies were invited for the big *Timb* singing and both the men and women of the village enjoyed that stage of the ceremony.

In the days that followed, the heavy rain ceased. Rain did fall but only in the night, so the villagers were able to plant their gardens. They all rejoiced in the fact that the goddess had accepted their sacrifice this time.

Months later, their gardens and livestock were doing so well, prompting Pombreol to announce to his family that there will be a thanksgiving sacrifice to the spirits of the ancestors called the 'Huwip Tomo'.

For that sacrifice a pig was to be selected and taken to their garden by the side of the river. The blood of

Pombreol

the pig was collected and poured on their crops by Pombreol, who was chanting praise and thankful words to the ancestors for all the blessings in their gardens and livestock. The rest of the family burnt some of the pork over open fires as a burnt offering.

It was soon becoming obvious that the clan was blessed abundantly with lots of food so that they had more than enough in every home. This pleased the chief so much that he wanted yet another sacrifice. This offering will be to the Sky Gods. He proudly announced his intention and tasked each family to collect all that is needed for this offering in few days' time.

On the day of the sacrifice called *'Yeki Toh'*, all gathered silently. The leaders of the sacrifice tied ropes from one tree to another. Smooth undergrowth in the forest called *'ti kwimb'* was tied to the rope so it provided a smooth pathway for the Yeki to come and visit the clan.

The village chief then called the Yekis by their names to visit them and accept their thanksgiving sacrifices. *"Yekiya kilamb, yekiya tossup"*, he shouted loudly, looking into the sky. Then the clouds came down and covered their food and vanished. The chief then concluded that their offering was accepted. The day was then ended with feasting on the pork leftovers and a celebration of dancing.

All was well for them now.

Twelve

MOONLIGHT HUNTING

By this time Pombreol had three sons and two daughters. Both his wives were in good health and he was surely strong enough to have several more sons. He also wanted to marry that other young girl too, but much of his wealth had been given to his mother's people, so he wouldn't. He took great pride in his three sons as he taught them carefully how to use the bow and arrow, do fencing, gardening, and so on. In the bright moonlight he would take them to hunt cuscus, wild pigs, and cassowaries in the thick bushes.

One such time he took his two older sons and set out late at night for the forest. His younger son asked him several times, wanting to go with them but they ignored him. After all he was still sleeping in the women's long house and as such he wasn't tough enough to stand the night's cold and its dangers.

With their little bundles they headed for the little bush hut built where men who went hunting could leave their extra things. Upon reaching their destination they left their raw *kaukau* pieces for next morning's breakfast and other unwanted things for the night, and walked in total silence to the big trees with hollows to hide in and wait for their animals.

As they sat quietly, with the two boys in one hollow and Pombreol in the next one, waiting patiently, there was a movement high up in one of the trees. All three pairs of eyes turned to that direction and were all sure it was a cuscus. They could smell the particular scent that a cuscus gives out. In between the moving leaves, they saw a huge cuscus feasting away on the leaves.

Automatically all three arrows pointed at the cuscus, ready to strike, when they heard the noise of a broken twig somewhere below. The cuscus suddenly disappeared behind the branches and leaves of the trees, as if sensing danger.

Pombreol cursed and swore silently at whoever made the disturbance, because it was said that if you have missed the first one, there would not be any kill for the whole night. Thinking of the wasted night, Pombreol was sure he would slaughter whoever or whatever broke that dry stick.

If it was a wild pig or a cassowary, he was sure they would have gone by now. If it was a tribesman he would surely pay for this. As they sat there starring into the night, always hoping for a catch, stiff with the night's cold, the two boys drowsed off. But Pombreol sat there like a piece of log not moving an inch trying his very best to keep his eyes opened as his eyelids involuntarily drooped.

In the quietness of the night, there was a sudden crashing noise and a shrill human cry from the shadow of the nearby ancient tree, followed by someone small running towards them with a very big wild pig charging right behind. Who could this be that the wild pig was almost devouring? And if it did catch him, the animal was big enough to swallow the little guy whole.

Pombreol stood very still as his eyes couldn't believe what was unfolding before him. Was it true? That boy was his younger son Naiko. By now, the other two boys were fully awake and for a while sat fixed to the tree as they watched their little brother, who was supposed to be at home, climbing up a huge tree as the wild pig was nearly upon him.

Terrified, as they watched not knowing what to do, the young boy somehow now managed to climb up the tree, but for some reason he fell down, this time right in front of the waiting pig. Before he had time to think Pombreol jumped down straight at the pig, attacking the pig with bare hands - he had dropped his arrow somewhere in the dark!

How did this boy conceal himself so well and follow them all the way? Anyway he would definitely need some answers if they both survived this!

Meanwhile the two boys up in the tree didn't know what to do as they watched helplessly as the pig charged straight for their father. As he looked around desperately for his spear, they could see that he would be dead in a short time. Seeing their father in great danger they too jumped down and started attacking the pig with their spear. By this time the younger son had found the father's spear and had brought it to him and, together, they all killed the wild animal.

"It's because of me that we killed this pig and today there will be a big feast in the village. You so called big boys didn't even kill anything and all through the night you were all hiding up there like women," boasted the younger brother.

Pombreol

Getting irritated with the little boy's boasting, one of the brothers asked, "Just how did you know we were hiding up there or that we did not kill anything?" Pointing to the dense undergrowth, he replied that he was lying under the covering after following them all the way.

Pointing up to a tree he said, "I saw a huge cuscus up there and as I sat up properly to see it, a dry stick broke under my foot and the next thing I knew the cuscus had disappeared."

The two bigger boys turned disbelieving eyes towards their father, who was already stiff with anger. They all understood now who had made the noise that had frightened the cuscus away earlier. Unaware of their glances the boy continued his tale, "As I continued to wait, this pig came out of the cave over there and came straight at me. Rest of the story you know."

"Listen son," said Pombreol, "you have done an unacceptable thing but you will tell me at home. For now, you will do us a great favour in keeping your big mouth shut and help us to tie this pig to take home as the day is dawning already."

When father spoke that way, it meant two things. Either Naiko would be tied to a tree or left alone overnight or he would be given no meal for the afternoon, with a good beating. Both of the punishments would be unacceptable because tied to a tree and left out overnight was a frightening experience - because of the stories that dead ancestors would come and give him more beating for being disobedient. Going without the meal would cost the pork meat that he had risked his very life for. He couldn't possibly miss out on that!

Thinking of all this, Naiko sadly walked behind, not even saying a word, while his father and brothers walked ahead with the load. He kept wondering why he followed them at all instead of staying behind. But if he had not gone, they never would have caught that pig. With a frown, he thought someone would make father understand that.

When Pombreol looked back he saw the kid frowning and walking very sadly. Without talking to any one in particular, he felt like laughing. He was always like that, talking to himself. Then he thought of how mature and brave he looked when the huge pig was charging him. His two big boys were strong but this one was stronger and he was sure of that. He was surely the one who was going to take his place.

Slowing his quick steps, he looked tenderly at him and told him to walk beside him. As they walked alone, Pombreol told him he was going to forgive him just this once. With a grin that totally lit up his face, Naiko looked up at his father with love and adoration and promised him never to do that again.

Back in the village everyone was excited about the pig and the women's stories went on forever about how it was killed, while the children hailed Naiko as a hero and the men folk marvelled at the tale.

All in all, Pombreol was sure the gods were smiling down on him since he was becoming successful in everything he did. His father would have been very proud of him. However, since his father was gone he wanted to give a thanksgiving offering to those unknown people who took care of the sky. He then gathered his wives and told them about his intentions. The family agreed on killing the white pig that was taken care of by Nawe's mother.

One fine sunny day he built his alter high above the ground. On the alter he collected a few stones and some

Pombreol

special bush leaves. He laid the stones on the altar and arranged the leaves on top of the stones. The raw heart which had been pulled out of the pig was placed on top of the leaves. As the family gathered below the altar, Pombreol climbed onto the altar and started raising both of his bloody hands into the sky in total surrender and worship of the sky beings. As the family below watched in total silence, he called out in a very clear loud voice in the silent air for those who live in the sky to accept his humble offering for making him a prosperous and happy man.

After the ceremony was over, he came down from the altar and assured his family that the offering was accepted and they could all go home and cook their pork. Only the raw heart was needed for the ceremony, so the rest they could party with.

Thirteen

THE SPIRITS MUST BE ANGRY AGAIN

Pombreol stood looking at his son Naiko who was bringing the news. "Hubin and the kids are coming with all their possessions. Something must have happened."

"Son what are you talking about?" he asked. He'd just returned from a hard day's work in the garden and was not up to jokes.

"Aunty and her children are all here with even their pigs," cried Naiko between breaths.

What on earth would they be doing here? His elder sister was married to a distant clan who were at least a day's walk away. Therefore if she was here with her things, something must have gone terribly wrong. Walking to the women's house, Pombreol found his sister there talking with his wives. Shaking his sister's hands in greeting and at the same time looking for some marks on her face in case her husband had beaten her, he asked them what brought them this far.

Pombreol

Greeting him, she said that in the village a lot of people had died with the deadly disease called *'okso'*. Therefore her husband sent them to stay with her people till things had settled down. Then he would come for them.

Pombreol couldn't believe his ears. His father had told him about this disease. It had claimed his own stepmother's life and lots of other people's lives, but he hadn't seen any in his time yet. From what he heard, a lot of people could die quickly after catching it. He just hoped it wouldn't come their way. However, it was nothing to worry about because it was affecting people in distant lands. Right now he told his wives to settle his sister and her children and he went to his house.

After some time, word went around that people were dying from the disease in the nearby village. The village chief, who by now was very old, told the people not to attend funerals because if flies touched them they would surely bring the disease into their own homes, which would be a disaster. Upon hearing this nobody attended any funeral in the nearby villages, even if a close relative died.

Despite all precautions and measures taken, several people from Pombreol's village caught the disease and Pombreol's heart was heavy with worry. They had buried one woman and a young girl already and more people were ill. Pombreol only hoped that his whole family was intact for he loved them all very much.

That night, Pombreol had a frightening dream. He was being chased by a wild and frightening pig and as he ran away, he fell into a deep pit, but nobody was there to help him. He woke up in fear and sweat and couldn't go back to sleep anymore. As he lay awake thinking about the dream, a few men were awake making a fire to get

Pombreol

warm, for the morning was very cold. Naiko burst into the house calling his father at the same time.

"Come quickly father. Big brother is not coming out of that toilet quickly. I have been waiting for my turn for a very long time and I can't control myself anymore," he exclaimed. "Where will I go? Maybe I'll go to the bush, but enemies might poison it and I might die." By now Pombreol was already making his way out, telling his son to shut up.

With a heavy heart Pombreol went to see what was going on because this could only mean one thing. His son had caught the disease! What he was dreading had at last entered his family.

Upon arrival he called out for his son. "Why are you sitting there so long?"

Standing tall next to his father and forgetting his urge to go to toilet, Naiko said maybe his big brother was just getting lazy not wanting to go to the garden.

"Naiko, you must shut up right now. I'm sure your brother must be very sick." When Naiko stopped talking, they could hear moans and groans from within the toilet house. Pombreol ran in and brought his now very floppy son out. He was in great pain.

"What's wrong with you?" asked a very tearful mum.

"I want to pass stool but not much is coming out except for a small hard one that I've passed hours ago with some fresh blood. I also have a very bad tummy ache and my head has been throbbing with pain all through the night and I haven't slept at all because of those aches and pains."

By now his whole family had gathered around him. "Nobody gets near him," ordered Pombreol. Sadly he took his son to an empty house where he was expected

Pombreol

to recover in isolation, attended to only by the village healer and his aid.

As Pombreol laid his hands on his son's forehead, he could feel it was burning with heat. "The boy is dying and he is being eaten by a spirit *(tomo)*. We must turn away the anger of the spirit or *tomo*," he said. So immediate preparation followed after Pombreol decided that a pig was to be offered to the dead ancestors for the sacrifice called the *'Tongte Tomo'*.

While the preparation of the firewood and leaves were going on, Pombreol went to a clearing and shouted for the people to come and take part in or witness the event.

The sick boy was then placed outside the house in the open air. The pig was then held by one man while another man bashed the pig's head again and again with a strong stick. They then hurried with the pig to a small spirit house built close to the dwelling area, and held it so that its blood flowed into a tiny hole in the ground. All the time this was going on, the men blew into the hole and very rapidly mumbled special words for the spirit to hear. When the pig ceased to struggle, it was taken away to prepare the pork for the people to eat.

A certain portion of the pork was given to the sick boy to eat, but he wouldn't as he was too sick. Therefore Pombreol ate it on his behalf. The rest of the people were not allowed to leave until the pig was all eaten up, as was the law about this kind of offering.

During the night that followed the sick boy showed no sign of recovery so the magic man talked to the spirit and asked what colour pig it wanted. According to the magic man, the spirit wanted the brown pig. It was decided that the brown pig be killed as a second offering in the morning and the whole procedure was all followed again.

The village healer also produced local stinging leaves and rubbed it on the boy's body but nothing happened. The village healer further slid the pig's kidneys onto a stick and cooked them over the open fire. Holding them close to the sick boy's head, he blew sharp breaths onto it, calling on the evil spirit to go out of the boy's body between every breath. Someone else also wrapped the blood-stained leaves around his chest and tied them on with lengths of bush rope.

By midday the sick boy was in total agony. There was nothing else the family could do as they watched in total silence. They had already brought other bush leaves and the mother, without fear, had gone in and rubbed them on his tummy and other areas where he had pains, but he had got worse. There was no sign of improvement and late in the evening he passed away. Pombreol couldn't believe it.

There was bitter weeping and wailing as people crowded around the dead boy. As an expression of her grief, his mother cut off the last finger of her left hand at the joint, while others gashed their ears with sharp bamboo knives.

After that more people were sick and others dying. It happened so fast that the people had no time to consult their gods. More than one member of a family died. All of Pombreol's children died, except Naiko and his wives, and he couldn't take this. He had given the best offering to the gods. Why should they take away his two big sons and his daughter? He felt like fighting with those responsible but he couldn't show his anger for fear of his own life too.

Pombreol

Pombreol wasn't feeling so good during those days, but he always thought it was because of all the mourning and sorrow. All his children had died and he could not even see them all dying let alone get out for their funeral. The vague weakness he had been experiencing was having its effect and the signs were that the deadly disease was catching up with him. He was anorexic, and losing all appetite for any food at all.

In the evening, four days after the burial of his young daughter, who was the last death in the family, his head was now throbbing severely with pain. He thought it was going to break open and all the contents spill onto the fireplace he was lying so close to, keeping his body warm.

That night his body was so hot and he was shivering so badly. In the dark night he could feel an ache somewhere deep down in his guts. He twisted, turned and moaned on his sleeping place, looking for a comfortable place to sleep as the pain increased. Who could help him now that his two big boy's sleeping places were empty and Naiko was still in the ladies house? The other tribesmen too were busy mourning and burying their own dead.

The men's house was the hardest hit by the disease. Men were heard groaning and moaning here and there. It was a terrible night as Pombreol lay in agony in the dark corner of his sleeping place.

Early in the quiet morning as the birds sing their morning songs, they sounded sad to his ears instead of what used to be bright and happy songs. Pombreol had an urgent desire to pass a stool so he crawled towards the toilet. As he sat there, pushing with whatever strength he had left, he felt like his head was cracking open with a kind of pain that he was sure he had never

ever experienced in his life before. He was sure he was going to die if the pain didn't stop.

Suddenly darkness closed in on him and he remembered nothing. He was sure there were some hands lifting him up and strange voices speaking but he was helpless even to open his own eyes. The last thing he remembered was falling helplessly into the deep pit that was in his dream the night before the death of his eldest son.

What was coming up at him? Was it a monster or witch? He could see it now, a living creature with two hands, one leg and one eye right on the forehead coming towards him. He could sense the evilness of the environment as the creature came straight at him with completely strange fingers, long nails aiming straight for his heart.

Oh, he had to escape somehow, but he was very weak and unseen hands were holding him down. He had to somehow fight it all for Naiko's sake. Who was going to bring him up if the frightening strange creature caught him?

Then he saw light on the other side of a river. There to his great joy he saw his father and his two sons. He forgot about his headache and shouted with all his might to them to come and help him, but they didn't seem to take notice of him, despite all his screams. How he wished with all his heart to be with them on the other side of the river and forget all about his troubles, but the river was too big to walk or even swim across, so he watched sadly as his loved ones walked out of his sight.

Then the darkness crept in again on him and the creature was back for him with what seemed to be his other friends. He needed to escape and started to run when strong hands held him down again. Darkness overtook him and this time he had no strength to fight it back so he couldn't do anything. He heard voices somewhere in the dark. Who was it now? He was sure he had heard that voice somewhere but couldn't remember where or when. He searched his brain but couldn't really remember.

All of a sudden the darkness lifted just like how it had appeared and that persistent voice was getting clearer. Yes, it was Naiko, his only surviving son and he was crying. Then he heard it all.

"Father, don't leave me alone. I don't know how I will move on in this world all alone; I have nobody to take care of me now." The cries were heart breaking and hold on - did he say there was nobody to take care of him? Surely his wives didn't die as well... he had to somehow open his eyes and comfort his son.

When at last he opened his eyes, he had a bad pain in his eyes therefore he closed them again. After a while he slowly opened his eyes again to find his son asleep at his side. He tried to turn on his side to have a look at his son better but his body was too heavy to do that. So he lay still studying his surroundings slowly as his eyes got used to the darkness and the environment around him became familiar.

It was now clear to him that he was lying down on his sleeping place in the men's house and that someone was making a fire in the fireplace. Several snores around him were heard.

Naiko, feeling that something was not right, opened his sleepy eyes forcefully and couldn't believe what they were seeing. The gods were cruel again to him playing silly tricks, or was he hallucinating? For the moment he didn't care. As long as this moment was not disturbed. His father was looking down at him with what he thought was a mixture of sadness and love in his eyes. But it couldn't be true for his father had not responded to anything for seven days now.

He hadn't responded even when he was told about the death of his two wives as well. Naiko was sure he was the only surviving member of his family but now that his father was waking up, he was sure it was a bad dream. But if somehow it was real, he just didn't know what to do, think or say. He truly was thankful to the gods for waking up his father.

Pombreol, forgetting about his fatigue, got up from his sick bed and hugged his son tightly, removing any doubts at all that Naiko had about whether his father was really alive. As a few surviving relatives gathered, he recovered fully within a few days.

Almost half of his clan members were all wiped out. How Pombreol was able to survive the ordeal was known only to the gods, if there were any gods at all. He also found out that out of his family, only Naiko and he were able to live through it. In fact, Naiko, along with a few others, had never contacted the disease at all. He realised too that his chance of becoming a village chief was slim as he had to start all over again.

After the mourning period was over and the funeral feast was done, Pombreol got himself a young widow with a young son from the neighbouring village. She had a son for him too but the child died when he was just crawling around. This made the mother so sad that she cut off the last finger to her left hand to show her great sorrow to the gods. Her next daughter died also.

Naiko was by now was growing up to be a very strong and attractive young man. Pombreol was very proud of him and told himself over and over again that when he looks for his bride she will have to be a hard working girl who definitely should come from a family that had lots of wealth.

One day, he and his friends went to attend a pig kill at the neighbouring village. Back from the party that afternoon, he went straight to bed complaining of tummy ache. In the night, the pain got worse and he started having diarrhoea and vomiting at the same time. Hearing his one precious son in agony, Pombreol couldn't stand it anymore. He then decided there and then that he was going to offer one of his pigs to the gods early next morning so his dear son got his healing.

The next day, Naiko was getting sicker so Pombreol told his clans men about his offering plan. They then arranged for one of his pigs secretly so that his wife and other ladies were not aware of what was going on because, for this particular offering, ladies were not supposed to know.

They took the big pig to the offering site, roasted it on the open fire and laid it on the altar. The men then painted themselves with white clay and started chanting special songs to wake up the angry ancestors to come for the peace offering. As they chanted away into the night, the usual signs of the presence of the dead ancestor's spirit was felt in the form of a whirlwind.

Everyone suddenly became quiet as the spirit medium went close to the sacrificial altar and talked with the dead ancestor's spirit. After much shaking and aggressive movement of his body and more chanting, he fell to the ground and laid motionless for a while before waking up.

When he woke up, the man walked towards the gathered men and told them that the spirits have accepted the gifts and that Naiko will be fine by tomorrow. With light hearts everyone travelled back to their house the next morning. However, upon arrival, Naiko had passed away and Pombreol cried like never before. Nobody could comfort him.

As people gathered for the funeral, men from the village watched the dead body carefully for any unusual sign appearing on the corpse which would mean the arrival of the person or tribes that caused the death. Nothing happened for a long time until the arrival of a few people from a village upstream, when the dead body opened his eyes and closed them again and suddenly there was bleeding from his nose.

After the second day of mourning the body was buried and men gathered to talk about the signs or *'puld'* of the corpse. The blame was all on the upstream tribesmen. They denied it but at the end they were Pombreol's tribesmens' bitter enemy, so nothing could be done about it. Pombreol knew why his son was dead. The magic was sent to kill him, but it got his son instead. He had too many enemies these days.

One day Pombreol developed a huge painful swelling to his right foot which disabled him from carrying out his daily activities. He and his cousin stayed indoors when his wife went gardening. Around noon, there was an unexpected shower of rain.

Pombreol told his cousin who was busy splitting firewood to follow him as this kind of rain was called the *'so sowep'* which was a sign of bad Oman. They crawled behind a huge tree and hide themselves there. Whispering to the young, curious cousin, Pombreol explained that this kind of rain with sun still shining would only mean one thing, and that is, a magic man was in their land.

Pombreol

After few minutes of waiting, they saw a very tall man arrive with his bow and arrow. The hidden two were surprised as the man who walked quickly towards the men's sleeping house was one of their own tribesmen, but belonging to a different subclan.

As they sat in total silence, the man came to a stop near the entrance and with a quick movement of his eyes looked around to make sure no one was around. Seeing no one, he hurriedly removed the door plug and went in. He was inside for a little while then came out, promptly looking around to make sure no one was about. He blocked the entrance with the wooden plug and quickly walked away. This was really strange as the man's subclan had their own sleeping house.

When the men of his subclan came home that afternoon, Pombreol told them what had happened and ordered the men not to enter the house until night. As night fell, all the men looked into the men's house and saw thousands of small lights glowing away innocently on Pombreol's bed. They then realised that the visitor was here to poison Pombreol. They got his sleeping mat and left it outside, while Pombreol shared his cousin's sleeping place.

The next morning the whole tribe was asked to gather, and Pombreol ask the man directly why he wanted to kill him. He denied all that was said until the sleeping mat was brought out and the man asked to lay on it. He flatly refused and the chief came to the conclusion that the accusation was true.

When asked again the man burst out that his mother's clan, who were the tribe's bitter enemies, promised him some wealth in exchange for Pombreol's life. They gave him the *'Tom Pe'* to pour on Pombreol's sleeping area so that he would be poisoned and killed.

The men were greatly angered and told him to leave their village for being a betrayer. They sent him away with his wives, children and livestock to stay in his mother's village as men were needed in that area.

Fourteen

DREAMS ARE NOT JUST DREAMS

Pombreol now was sure that the god of his clan's favour was not on him because he had lost all his wives and children of his youth. His latest wife was still alive but her two children too had died. He couldn't take it anymore. With a heavy heart he gathered his people and announced that he was going away forever to his mother's village over the mountain as he had talked with his uncles and they were willing to give him land.

The people couldn't believe it. "Who was going to be their great warrior or even take the chief's position?" someone asked. "What does it matter if a man has no children to take over his wealth, title or position?"

A tearful and out of control Pombreol burst out as the reality of all the recent sorrowful events hit him hard.

"All my children and wives are gone and my life has been nothing but a life of distress, grief and sadness. These have been my everyday experience and I cannot take it anymore. All my pigs have been offered to the gods but either the gods are angry with me or there are no gods at all. I am a man leaving this land for my mother's land in desperation and hopelessness," he lamented on and on until everyone present had tears in their eyes. "I only hope that the god that my uncles worship is more kind as I start afresh at this age, hoping that something good comes out of life".

"I really am a man in deep sorrow as I have lost all that I held dear to my heart," he continued. "I really think I am in a bad dream and that soon I will wake up to find everything just as it was. My children playing around the house cheerfully and their mums busy in the gardens, looking after pigs and cooking in the house, that is what it was like and that is what I want. I would give up anything for this kind of life to come back".

After his bitter speech, the chief and the villagers farewelled him, telling him he was welcome back to his village anytime.

Therefore Pombreol was in his middle age when he left his clan to join his mother's clan. When he and his wife with their livestock, consisting of a female and two male pigs, and their few belongings arrived at his mother's village, he was well received by his uncle who had no children of his own. He was then given land to build his own house and make gardens.

His wife conceived no more so they decided to buy a new bride. The plan was then made known to the uncle and the clan members, who quickly agreed to pay the bride price for any young woman he preferred. His preference was the young woman who had danced so gracefully with him but slipped away unnoticed. Pombreol had made it his business to find her whereabouts. She was Nalomnong, the daughter of a chief from downstream.

Pombreol

After much negotiation over the bride price with her relative from downstream, a generous amount was paid by his mother's people and he brought the young bride home. She comforted him in all his sorrows and pain and he began to love her so much. After some time, his young wife fell pregnant, his livestock had become productive again, and Pombreol was sure he was recovering from his losses and was doing well again. Pombreol was sure his mother's clan's god had welcomed him as well. All was going well for him as he settled in his mother's land.

One fine moonlight night, he went hunting up in the hills. As he got closer to the dense forest, everything was so unusually quiet, he stopped himself abruptly and stood straight up and stared into the somewhat shadowed track. For some reason he felt his body hair rising and he was shivering with fear from an unknown cause. He felt that someone was watching him from within the thick forest and fear gripped him so hard that he wanted to shout out. But no words came out of his opened mouth. He didn't know what to do.

As he stood there like a shaking leaf, a creature stood before him in the moon light. One side of the creature's body was human while on the other side, trees, grass and the undergrowth of the forest had grown. Pombreol by now had lost control of his bladder and felt urine dripping down his cold legs.

He knew who this was. It was his mother's clan's forest god, as described to him by his mother when he was a small boy, and now more recently by his uncles. Now fragments of what his mum told him about this creature came into his mind. Part of it was that this creature appears rarely to mankind and once you have seen him you have to grab him so you get your wish from

Pombreol

him. Pombreol, forgetting all fear, rushed forward and grabbed hold of him but the creature had turned into a rock which then turned into a tree. He kept holding onto it until he realised he was holding onto the empty air. *'Berkesail'*, the forest owner, had disappeared. Pombreol walked home in disappointment without a cuscus or a wish made to the forest god.

Back home he explained to his uncle what had happened. His uncle told him that he appeared only to welcome him into the mother's clan and Pombreol can be sure no harm will come his way as long as he remains in his mother's village.

Fifteen

INTO THE HANDS OF THE ENEMY

Pombreol's clan was over the mountain and so once in a while he would visit his relatives and come back. One such time he told his wives that he was going to visit his clansman. He got his bow and arrows and was on his way when he met a very handsome man on the road. Seeing that he was a stranger Pombreol greeted him.

After they had exchanged a few words of greetings, the stranger asked if he knew a man by the name of Pombreol who was from over the mountains but had come to live in his mother's village.

"Why do you ask for Pombreol or where he lives?" asked Pombreol, without showing any surprise or sign that he was the man that this stranger was seeking.

"Because I hear he lives somewhere around here and I do not want to accidently meet him. His clan is my tribe's worse enemy and his big son was killed by magic by my own father, so I am scared of what he might do to me as he is a popular warrior who fears no men," the man said.

"It's common knowledge among my tribesmen that he had buried a stone near his son's grave vowing to kill one man from my tribe in exchange for his one son, who had survived even the sudden plague that had attacked and killed a lot of people, but was killed by magic by my father."

Pombreol almost fainted when he realised the luck coming his way. He could feel anger slowly growing deep down in his belly and rising up to overcome him and almost chocking him to death as he remembered how Naiko suffered such a very short illness and died. Anyway, for now he had to control that or the stranger will sense something.

Pombreol smiled kindly at the stranger and told him that the Pombreol that he is scared of lives across the river in the next village along the road he was following. So, if he wanted to avoid him, he must follow another track leading to his own village. The stranger eagerly followed the path directed by Pombreol.

As the stranger took the path that avoids the enemy's village and arrived at the road junction as advised, there was a man standing behind a huge tree. When the man came into the open he recognised him to be the person who had shown him the smaller track. He then asked the man how he arrived at this spot before he did since he had left him behind.

"Listen carefully," said the man, "because this maybe the last time you hear something, I am the one called Pombreol and I have arrived here faster with this for you." Before the stranger knew what was happening Pombreol shot him in the heart at close range and the

Pombreol

stranger fell to his death. Pombreol felt a great burden lifted from his heart as he, with his own hands, killed the son of the very man who killed his son.

After he was dead, Pombreol got help from some of the men from his mother's clan and took the body to the mountain top where he called down to his enemies to collect their 'animal', and left the corpse there. When Pombreol's clansmen heard what had happened, they celebrated the whole day. They were happy that he went to live over the mountains so he could kill enemies like that.

Two days after celebrating the revenge, Pombreol got up early and went back to his wives and found that his little son by the young wife was having some difficulty in breathing and his little body was very hot. With a heavy heart he asked the mother if she had taken the baby to some sacred place, to which she replied negative. He also asked if a few of the ladies who are thought to be practicing witchcraft had seen the baby, but the answer was still no.

After much discussion they came to the conclusion that the baby was sick because Pombreol didn't give any wealth to the mother's relatives in appreciation. Pombreol quickly arranged for two very big pigs and a bamboo container full of oil, and gave it away to the baby's uncles, who accepted gratefully. Despite the giving away of wealth the little fellow got hotter and died a few days later.

Pombreol by now was so sad. Nothing he ever did was helping his family. If there was anything at all he could do to save his family, he knew he would gladly do it and that was it. In desperation he felt like he really needed to get an answer from some extraordinary people, but he just didn't know where or how.

No time to catch up with those thoughts, for his mother's clan's biggest feast called the *'sai da'*, was being prepared. This was the most important of all feasts, for people from near and far would gather and judgment would be passed on who had slaughtered the biggest, fattest and largest number of pigs.

Relatives are invited from near and far, including young girls who have gone to marry elsewhere. For them this was the time to show whether they had rich relatives or not, and whether those relatives cared for them at all by giving them a quarter or half a pig.

Pork would also be cut and given according to what they have received when the other clans did their feast. Pombreol was sure to get a lot of shares as this was his mother's village and he had given them big shares when he killed pigs back in his father's village.

Stones, firewood, leaves and fern had been collected weeks earlier and left in the big gathering place called the *'homah'*, left in order of family groups and sub-clans cooking places.

Word was sent to relatives near and far of the time of the events. Where relatives were hard to contact, signs were set up with white banana stems called the *'mark hall'* on well cleared hills so relatives leaving from distant lands could see the signal, and know some important events were taking place in their relative's village, and come. That has always been the best way of sending emergency messages. And so people started pouring in a few days before the pig kill, and the village was filled with people.

Young girls from the village who were engaged would also have their relatives giving them all the stuffed and cooked pig's stomach, with several quarter pigs to the boy's relatives. They were helped by other young girls

Pombreol

and mothers. This ceremony called the *'ol da'* would strengthen the relationship between the two young people and their relatives.

Pombreol's cousin sister had a boyfriend from the next village and the men from that clan had asked the girl to bring some pigs, so they were getting ready for that as well. Pombreol would give one of his quarter legs to her and her father and his brothers would give her several of them. She and the other ladies will take them to his village.

When they were talking about the ceremony and seeing his cousin's shy face, Pombreol remembered how a girlfriend of his brought some pork and pork bellies to his village when his father was still alive. He was a very young and handsome man then. When the clansmen were gathering some wealth to pay for the pork, his other girlfriend who he loved very much somehow got the word that women were bringing pork as *'ol da'* to Pombreol's house. Suddenly she and the women from her village arrived in the village and smashed those pork pieces up with big sticks. Then the other group retaliated and that afternoon there was a big fight over him. He remembered hiding in the bush in shame until both ladies were sent away by his clansmen. This brought a smile to his face but right now he had to collect his last minute decoration materials from the bush.

A few days before the event, the men decorated themselves and traditional singing, dancing and chants came alive during the day. Courting among the young boys and girls in the night gave the ceremony the desired flavour.

After two days of singing and dancing to the beat of the kundu drums, on the final day before the feast the pigs for the feast were displayed for judgment by the general public in the gathering place. All the pigs were then lined up from the biggest to the smallest for other clansmen to see. Comments were made that this was one of the biggest pig kills, and an important announcement was made by the chief.

Very early the next day, the cries of pigs in agony were heard all over the land as they were slaughtered the highlands way. Excited kids were already up fighting for the pigs' ears, for this was the first part to be roasted over the open fire and eaten. The air was now polluted with burning pig's hair. More pigs were being killed while others were being butchered, and those that had been butchered already were being lined up on a big log prepared especially for that. Men were free to give their opinions on which pig was the biggest and fattest.

The internal organs of the pigs were prepared well and shared among the invited guests to cook and eat before the pork meat was cooked. Almost all those who were killing pigs were calling Pombreol's name for the raw internal organs he will get as his share of pork from those people only. Everyone knew he was getting the largest number of shares. After all, this was his mother's village and his uncles do love him. As people roasted some over the fire and cooked others in bamboo containers before heating the stones for the *mumu*, there was more than enough.

Suddenly, above all the noises that were going on was another strange kind of noise coming from somewhere. Pombreol, who was very good at hearing things even from a distance, heard this strange noise and suddenly stopped what he was doing and looked around. He was about to tell those who were within hearing distance about this strange noise when he realised that everything had suddenly gone silent, except for the explosive bangs from the new river stones which were being heated over the open fire for the *mumu*.

The weird noise was getting closer and clearer. People looked around in total confusion to see what it was that was making this extraordinary noise and where it was coming from. By now people were sure it was coming from the sky but they were not sure why the sky would make such a funny noise.

Then some brave person out in the crowd broke the silence and commented that the sky gods may want some pork too. Then people added all sorts of comments, and the concentration of the minute's fearful silence was lost. The men went back to their duties again.

Then to their dismay, the peculiar noise was heard again, and this time the noise was very loud. Pombreol thought it was evil too. As the odd sound got persistently louder, all the people present were sure the sky was breaking open. No one dared to look up. After all, who had the guts to be face to face with the sky gods? A new kind of terror was felt among the people as they forgot about their pork and found refuge in the sanctuary of some huge trees and other protective coverings.

Most of the people who were unable to reach shelters lay flat on the ground, closing their ears with both of their hands, trying to block off the evil noise. Others who were able to run, ran for their dear lives, forgetting all their precious pork. There was great confusion among everybody.

As people ran into each other in total confusion, there was only one man who had the guts to look up and that was Pombreol. He surely had some unfinished business with those gods. Evil weird noise or not, he had a few unanswered questions for those damn gods, for they were the reason for his bitter life. They had taken many of his loved ones after he had lived to please them.

If only Naiko was still alive he wouldn't be so bitter. But now that he was gone, just like the others, it really did not matter if he came face to face with those gods with the evil and deafening noise. He really needed to see what kinds of gods they were, so he looked up with bitterness in his heart when he was sure the noise was right above them.

As he kept his eyes on the spot where the noise was coming from, he saw it, whatever it was. It was a huge shining bird flying straight toward him with that deafening noise. If it were a god, it had to be the god of the birds because the thing looked like a huge bird flying over the tree tops.

The noise itself was wicked. Terrified men ran in all directions trying to get as far away from the beast and its noise. Men were never coming back, not to this evil village. Not for a very long time. The strange big bird with the evil and bizarre noise went on its way and those who heard about it were terrified. People decided not to talk about it fearing it might appear again.

Sixteen

STRANGE HAPPENINGS

It had been some time since the big shining bird with the evil noise had gone over the village, but it was not easily forgotten. Mothers used this event to threaten their children when they were lazy or not doing their chores. Upon hearing this, children would carry out their task without putting up much resistance, for fear of being carried away by the evil bird with the unforgettable noise. The mothers told them this would happen if they disobeyed their parents.

By now, Pombreol's last wife's daughter named Sanowi was the only living child he had. He gave her that name because the gods had taken away all his children and wives. This girl may not be alive for long either, so he may as well not count her. So the name meant 'not counted'.

This daughter however was very active as she followed her dad around wherever he went. Despite the name he had given her, Pombreol began to be very proud of her as she was even beginning to do boy's jobs. Because he had no boys to bring up, he taught her anywhere. He just couldn't help it. After all, she was his only living child. If only she were a boy his happiness would be full.

One particular bright morning, men from the clan all decided to dig a drain on a swampy area to plant taro. They worked hard the whole morning. Kids brought them drinking water and women brought them their usual lunch of sweet potato cooked in ashes and greens cooked in bamboo. Pombreol and his men took a short break for lunch and continued to work.

As the sun heated their bare brown bodies, each man was so hard at work that nobody seemed to notice the noise that was slowly coming towards them. Suddenly, above all the noise of the digging sticks and the other men at work, the deafening noise was heard again.

Pombreol, who stood up very stiff and straight, called out in a sharp voice, "What's that noise?" His voice was so strange that everybody looked across to where he was standing. But almost immediately, they looked away in the direction of the peculiar noise which they too had just heard.

Completely puzzled, they all stood listening intently. When the men looked up and saw this evil force with that horrifying noise floating very low over the tree tops towards them, they all knew. This was the thing they saw during the feast, which was a forbidden topic in the village.

Then Pombreol shouted in a voice in which there was sheer terror. "Look! A huge bird! We are all doomed!" And before the shock of what they were seeing could draw upon all of them, Pombreol turned and fled into the bush. Everyone dropped their working tools and ran in all directions in pure terror. Nobody had to warn anybody. Even those who had not looked up to see knew what it was. They ran for their dear lives.

Pombreol

As Pombreol took refuge by a tree, he stood his ground but his knees were knocking together with fear. The children had rushed to their mothers for protection, but he was terrified to see his daughter, who as usual had gone with him, stuck in the swamp struggling to get free.

Suddenly, her small voice was heard above the silence. "Look father, some things are falling from the sky." Nobody dared to go out of their hiding place to expose themselves, but as she was only a small girl perhaps she could just be seeing things?

However she wasn't giving up as her persistent voice became shrill, and Pombreol, without thinking, ran out of his hiding place and looked up into the direction that his daughter was pointing. He saw objects falling out of the sky and, not believing what he was seeing, stared into the sky in total confusion and horror. He had never felt fear like this in all his lifetime, not even in the battle fields when his life was in danger, or during his trading days when he was passing through enemy land. This fear was starting up from right within his bones so that he felt so weak he didn't know what to do.

Seeing Pombreol in such a state, the men all ran from their hiding places into the clearing, looking up at the sky at the same time. Seeing what had made Pombreol so scared, they stood in great amusement as they watched the things forming shapes. Pombreol saw a whole lot of things falling out from that strange bird, but what were those things, he wondered?

The things were coming down very fast and soon they would be showered in those things. They must escape from those things or they will all be killed. The men gathered the little strength they had left and ran in all directions, the women doing the same thing from wherever they were. Pombreol grabbed Sanowi and ran straight for the cave. Sanowi's mum was heavy with pregnancy therefore she was way behind as all the people rushed for the big cave which had always been their hiding place from their enemies. From there they could see a long way and also see their enemies coming too. There was also a crevice in the rock where they could all hide and feel safe.

The great silvery bird, making a deafening noise, had its two wings spread wide and was rushing through the sky above them. Pombreol was not sure whether it had seen them or not, but it appeared to take no notice and sped on its way, disappearing into the blue sky as mysteriously as it had come.

As everyone huddled inside the cave, not even a single noise was heard. Even the babies seemed to understand there was something unusual going on and were quiet. After a long silence, the village chief spoke everyone's thoughts aloud.

"Strange and sinister things have been happening in this village," he said.

"Like the big bird with the evil noise that disturbed our party and celebrations months ago," someone contributed.

"That was the same bird today," someone else added.

Then everyone started talking without raising their voice at once. They all didn't know what to do. This was nothing like their tribal warfare, or the witch doctors consulting the dead. This was totally strange even to their ancestors. And so, that afternoon, the whole valley echoed and re-echoed with endless talk about the sky bird.

Pombreol

As the sun disappeared behind the ridge that evening, Pombreol stood on the entrance of the cave deep in thought, his gaze wandering backwards and forwards again and again into the blue sky into which the great bird had gone.

Is it coming back again? If it does, will it harm him and his people? Did the people of the other clan see it or is it just appearing to his tribesmen only? Is it one of the sky spirits? These were some of the unanswered questions in his mind. After all, how was he to know that a new era was dawning for his people!

He knew that no one in the group, including the village chiefs, elders and magicians, had the answer to those thoughts. When it came to that bird with the evil noise, no one seemed to have any answer. In reality it drove them into an unexplainable fear.

It would be a spell being cast upon them by the sky gods that's terrorising them with such fear, he thought, and walked back to the silent group still frightened. Then he shivered and, realising it was very chilly and darkness was approaching, hurried towards them. They all lay huddled together in the cave that night as nobody wanted to leave the safety of the cave. A fear so powerful grabbed hold of even the strongest men of the village.

As he lay there, Pombreol found it hard to sleep. His mind wondered about all these strange happenings. Not even his father had prepared him for this, so he didn't know how to fight back. The next day dawned just like any other day and so Pombreol and the people went back to their homes.

Seventeen

HUMANS OR GODS???

It was impossible to forget that the god of the sky had come and visited them twice already, but months passed by and it did not appear again. Pombreol then decided that the most recent visit after the first was the last time they would ever see the sky bird with the most terrifying sound. The thing was never coming back again and he said so to his family.

He then picked up his bow and arrows and started fixing the curves of the arrow with his expert hand. At least he had his fighting gear ready, if those sky spirits come back again. He will definately shoot at someone this time. After all, he was not a great warrior for nothing.

Pombreol and his people teased each other and sometimes laughed at each other for running away and hiding that day. Each person, including the children and very old people, had their own stories to tell. As they settled back to their normal life, someone would suddenly laugh and give his or her tale of what had happened - how they took flight in fear leaving all their fighting weapons behind.

Pombreol

One such tale was when one of the young men climbed up a tree to hide. But when he realised that the sky bird was flying very low and straight at him, he jumped down in fear and twisted both of his ankles. In great pain he crawled all the way to the hiding place. Everyone would burst out in more laughter when someone else, who was also fleeing and had seen him jump down and crawl around in agony, then imitated what he had seen, presenting it before the whole group. The actor would then cry in more pain and add some of his own imagination to add flavour to his stories, resulting in more laughter. The victim would then swear at the actor for the extra action which was obviously added to embellish the story for the group. It really was fun.

Pombreol then hoped it would never come back again. He was getting tired of talking about the strange bird and decided to go to Noweamenda to look for firewood. His daughter Sanowi decided to follow him to look for and collect mushrooms in the bush. As they walked to the top of the mountain both father and daughter were out of breath and perspiring. The road was steep and narrow and going uphill on this particular mountain was hard. They could both hear each other's laboured breathing as they lay down on the soft grass on the very top of the mountain.

The trail below was crooked, winding and dangerous but leading to the most amazing view. He was always glad when he made it to the top. He would view the valley, but for now he needed to rest for a while.

Pombreol had then drifted off to sleep for a moment and woke up with a start to find that the merry young girl had gone into the nearby bush and was already filling her net bag with mushrooms she had collected. Having his strength renewed, he strolled across to the top of the mountain and sat himself comfortably on top of a piece of unmoveable rock that had been used as seat by all who were lucky enough to get to the top of mountain. Oh, how magnificent it was to be on top of this high mountain!!!

No matter how spectacular the valleys were, the mountains always attracted him and this was where he always had his strength renewed. From where he sat, he could look across the whole valley. As he sat there quietly and gracefully looking across the valley, he was taken aback by the beauty of it all.

The valley was like a sleeping giant silently staring back at him, and he gleefully stared back at it in awe. The valley was so green with its ancient rivers flowing down freely from their source, joining the mighty river that flows in the southern part of the valley. He didn't need to know where that mighty river carried the smaller ones to. For now he was just content with what he was seeing.

Pombreol was grateful. He had to climb up the hardest track to the mountain to see the beauty of the world of nature which was all presented before his very own eyes to feast on. He was indeed grateful to the Great Spirit who created them for him and his children to use. As his eyes feasted on all the endless valleys, hills, woods, fields and the steep mountains near and far, he was proud that he was from this great land, and hoped that peace, harmony and beauty would reign supreme over the land as it was now.

For this land, he, Pombreol, would fight anyone, including the sky gods, to his last breath.

He was still thinking about that and looking down the valley in total admiration when he thought he saw something strange and sat up straight. There it was, he saw a fine column of smoke rising up in the eastern side of the forest close to his village. He rubbed his eyes hard to make sure he was not seeing thing. But surely the smoke from the fire rising innocently forever and ever into the clear blue sky in the stillness of the valley must have been built by someone other than his tribesmen. His clansmen can't be doing this because this portion of the land was sacred. Only men go there for special clan offerings once in a while.

This was within their border and his tribesmen's offering ground. He was sure nobody had gone there today. It was an untouched forest so nobody was making gardens there either. He would have known if some special offering was going on. Suddenly he felt a shiver run down his spine and, despite the hot sun, he was shaking like the leaves in the nearby bush, shaking by the force of the gentle breeze.

Rubbing the sudden appearance of sweat from his forehead, he felt in his bones that this was no ordinary fire. He needed to alert his tribesmen but he couldn't shout down as he was sure whoever was making fire would hear him. Therefore he gathered his bow and arrows, screamed at his daughter to follow, and ran down the hill.

Sanowi was not happy with this sudden change of plans as there were more mushrooms to be harvested, but she had no choice. Following her father down the steep hill was even harder on this part of the way and she slid and fell, getting up quickly to keep up with her father's fast steps. What was the big rush? Why he was not even carrying his firewood which was the very reason for this trip? Why did he look like he had just seen a ghost? After all, ghosts do not appear to people in bright daylight but only in the night, so this has to be something else.

With these questions still running through her mind she too walked as fast as her little legs would carry her. The fear that he might have seen a spirit did not explain why he was running so fast. He did look like he saw something that affected him so much - the fear on his face was like the fear she saw the time he had seen the sky bird.

For sure, there was no sky bird, so this time it must be a ghost that walks around aimlessly in broad daylight out in the thick bush only. With that thought she ran faster, quickly looking back at the road to see if the ghost that frightened her dad to the core of his being was following them. Upon reaching her father she dared not ask any question for fear of the answer, therefore followed his quick footsteps in total silence. Once or twice she got tackled by a twig or a vine and fell down but she did not make any noise, quickly got up and kept running until they reached the safety of the village.

Upon reaching the village, they both fell on the grass, panting like dogs. Someone offered Pombreol water which he waved aside, while another asked Sanowi what really was the matter. She had no answer. Now the number of people gathered around them was growing quickly. Someone else asked him if he was sick and if not, what was the matter? He didn't answer that either. Finally, as though with a great effort, he looked at each of those gathered around him and told them he had seen smoke rising up from their scared land where their offering house stands. The whole group with one accord stared at him in total silence. One of the elders, who had a mouth full of sweet potatoes, choked, and someone standing near him had to slap him on the back so he did not have to cough so much, disturbing the rest of the people.

"Which land are you talking about?" This question came from the now ageing chief of the village. Without further words, Pombreol pointed towards the eastern side of the village. All eyes followed Pombreol's pointed fingers and, to their uttermost surprise, there was the smoke rising forever into the sky. This was a no go land and even the children knew that. Who in the world could go to a sacrificial ground where all the strong spirits live and make fire away?

Everyone was speechless and stood transfixed where they where. There was smoke rising in an area that belonged to them, yet no one in the tribe had any idea about who in the whole wide world had invaded their sacrificial ground. Even their enemies would avoid such lands because they were not powerful enough to fight with the spirits. Who on earth would be making fire out there? Real confusion and fear was evident on everyone's face. The strangest things have been happening in this valley. What with the strange silver bird and now fire in the most sacred area? Whispering to each other, the people gathered their few belongings and took refuge again in the cleft of the rock towering above their village.

Meanwhile a few brave men were assigned to collect food stuffs, for it was agreed that nobody was to come out of their hiding place until they knew exactly what was going on. When the men returned, everyone gathered around anxiously to gather as much information as possible, but nothing new was heard.

Pombreol

That night in the cold cave, men talked about the best way to find out about the happenings in the forest. After much discussion well into the night, it was decided that a few men would be sent as spies to the area where the smoke was seen rising the day before. Therefore a few of the bravest men of the tribe were selected, including Pombreol.

As the selected group set out in the morning, the rest of the people waited anxiously in their cold hard cave, except for Sanowi. She was crying softly, hiding behind her mother's back, fearful of what might happen to her dad. She didn't have the nerve to cry aloud though.

Pombreol led the way as they crept forward, sliding and crawling in some instances. Nobody dared to say a word or make any noise. They travelled this way for a while until Pombreol came to a stop suddenly with his right hand up indicating they should stop and listen. Everyone stopped to listen intently. They could all hear the noise of chopping wood. In the still morning air, the noise seemed so loud, sending a shiver down each man's spine.

With hearts beating fast, they listened some more as all kinds of thoughts ran through their minds. This land belonged to them and their ancestors so who would be chopping wood as if they had every right to do so. If this fellow thought he was going to escape with this, he might as well think twice about it because the bravest and the strongest men of this land were here to challenge him. Right now they had their bows and arrows ready and aimed at the culprit.

All of a sudden the leading man stood fixed to the spot and the one after him almost collided with him. As Pombreol, the leading man, motioned for them all to come beside him, they couldn't believe what was

Pombreol

unfolding before their very eyes. There was the strangest of men chopping firewood with something like one of their precious stone axes except that his was very sharp. In an instant he had chopped enough firewood to last several days.

All stood together and stared and stared - this fellow was the strangest of human beings. No wonder he had fallen out of the sky. His body was all covered up too. Stranger still, his stone axe was the sharpest on earth for, in the short time that they were there, he had chopped enough firewood to last a life time. At this rate everyone was sure their firewood would finish.

Nobody had the guts to make a move or even say a word, let alone use their bows and arrows, for they had never seen any human like that. They could be shooting at the devil himself without even knowing it!

As they watched in total silence, there was a movement and they could see someone like the first man coming out of a totally weird covering that seemed to have some kind of door that was facing them. He walked up to his friend and they were both talking in an absolutely bizarre language, and then he disappeared in the opposite direction.

As Pombreol and his men hid in the canopy of the nearby trees, creating enough space so all could see clearly, they didn't know what to do except gaze and gaze at the extraordinary person. They had momentarily forgotten their bows and arrows as the human that disappeared in the opposite direction walked out of the forest straight towards them, spotting Pombreol and his men. The men ran back the way they came in real terror, wetting themselves with their own urine all the way to the cave.

Pombreol

As soon as they reached the cave, everyone began to talk as the people waiting gathered around them, anxious and eager for more news. In between breaths, Pombreol decided to recall what they had seen out in their very own forest.

Pombreol blinked his eyes hard, rubbed them with his hard fist and then began his incredible story.

"Except that we saw them with our own eyes, we could not believe it," he began. "We were hiding to spy on them, and there they came straight at us. First the sky bird, now two strange human beings. For a moment we wanted to run away but could not move. We could only sit there and watch him as he approached us. Before he got any closer, we got up and ran for our dear lives."

"What did they look like?" urged Sanowi, her hands pulling at her father's arms, only too eager to have her father back safely.

"The one who was approaching us was very tall and big and white. His eyes were blue and hair pale and straight." Pombreol looked down on his daughter leaning on his knee and moved his hand thoughtfully over her short tight brown curls.

Someone else picked up the tale and told the gathered people that their bodies and legs and feet were covered with some kind of clothing which was nothing like ours. The hardest part to explain was the humans they saw out there running around in their forest. After answering the chief's questions, the people gathered around to make more plans as to how to go about solving this very difficult situation.

After some discussions it was decided that a second group be sent the next day, again to spy on the strangers. This second group brought the same news. Sadly they realised whoever was out there was here to stay.

Pombreol

Since they could not stay in the hard cold cave forever, the people were advised by their chief to move back to the village. He again announced that the strangers had been in the forest for several days but no harm has been done to them, therefore they could all go to the comfort of their own houses while plans are underway to solve the issue.

That afternoon the chief gathered his people, this time in the village. He told them that whoever was out in the forest in their land wasn't forgotten. He and his warriors would think of a way to get rid of them but meanwhile everyone was encouraged not to leave the safety of their village and that they must always go out to food gardens in groups.

Early the next morning the sound of tribal warfare was heard in the neighbouring villages. Not knowing which two clans were fighting, everyone waited for news in great anticipation. By noon time there wasn't any news and no more war cry was heard, so Pombreol and his men decided to walk to that village to find out for themselves.

When they arrived at the village they couldn't believe what they saw. Lying in a pool of blood in the middle of a crowd was a man like the one they saw in their forest, lying face down. The complete stranger was indeed dead.

The crowd was quickly getting bigger but there was total silence. As they gazed at the body in total fear, the story came out. The man and others like him had come a few days earlier. The tribesmen had kindly asked them to leave their village but they did not, so he was shot with bows and arrows and later beaten to death while the others escaped.

As Pombreol looked closely, he saw that the corpse had no toes and his whole body was so wrapped up that his strange white fingers and his head and face were the only parts that made him look human. His hair was also very short yet didn't look like hair at all. Actually it looked like the soft tip of a corn plant. The body was so strange. He remembered the teaching that was handed down by his father to him from the generations.

"One day a strange man will arrive on this land, he will have no toes and you won't see his body either, yet he will be human. If you ever live to see that man, things will never be the same."

And now with a loud pounding heart that was about to explode in his chest, Pombreol realised that this was the day and the time. It was his time and things will never be the same again. Those beings had come from somewhere and he was sure they would come for revenge.

When the strangers returned the next day, it was with more men, but they did not seem to have any weapons except a funny shaped piece of wood that only a few men seemed to carry by their sides. However, the Poes tribe had been prepared for that. They had asked all the men from the nearby tribe to help them and Pombreol and his uncles readily agreed, for they needed to gather with as many warriors as possible if they were to drive these strangers off their land.

The Poes tribe and the rest of the helping warriors quickly agreed that they should use the stranger's body as a bait to trap the rest of his friends. They all quickly armed themselves and hid in the bush, leaving the body in the open space. They were still waiting there when the strangers came back again with their strange piece of wood.

As they approached the body, a man called Poes Tommie got out of his hiding place with his bow and arrow firmly aimed at the stranger. Before he had a

Pombreol

chance to shoot someone, one of the strangers quickly lifted his strange wood at him, producing the loudest bang. In the blink of an eye Tommie's guts were spilt all over the ground right in front of his hiding tribesmen and the helping tribes.

Hidden men ran in all directions without even looking back, let alone assisting their fallen comrade. After meeting together at the top of the hill, Pombreol and his men walked quietly home, each man lost in his own thoughts. Back in their village when the chief asked about the success of the trip, each men was lost for words as the events of the day were hard to explain. Neither they nor their forefathers had seen anything like this.

In the next few days more of those strange white men, and other men who were looking like them but with a strange smell and coverings that totally hid their skin, were going through all the villages in that area looking for any men, women and children who belonged to the Poes' clan.

However, every one of them had been hidden by other surrounding tribes in the forest and caves. Words were quickly passed around that no tale was to be told about the hidden people, so the brave men decided not to expose their neighbours. More distressing news too was that Poes Tommie's body was not allowed to be taken for burial, so it was left there to decay.

In Pombreol's village, the bravest men got Poes Homelem and Poes Paikeyem, the two sisters of Poes Tommie, and hid them in one of their sacrificial houses, as the strangers were hunting for these two girls everywhere in the land. They knew they were breaking their rules for women not to enter a sacrificial house

Pombreol

but they didn't know any other better place than their ceremonial house to hide the two beautiful sisters.

When the strangers were away continuing their search in the next village, the men would provide food and water for the two sisters. The next day, the strangers were always back. Pombreol and his men knew there was a tip off somewhere but they never exposed the two hidden girls until the search was put off.

As soon as the search was called off, Poes Homolem and Poes Paikeyem were brought out from their hiding place and sent back to their village. The two very grateful girls walked back to their village with their own clansmen who came to pick them up.

In Pombreol's village nobody wanted to talk about the strangers in their own forest, for in their very hearts they knew they were overpowered. They had witnessed all that had happened to the Poes Tribe and the power and destruction that those strangers carried around in a piece of wood - enough to spill human guts on the ground immediately with the strangest, loudest bang. They would never know whether it was magic or something else.

The one thing that gave them peace was that those in their forest seemed harmless to them as none of them came near them or threatened them at all in anyway. They had only gone to spy on them and when they were caught, they always ran back. Those men never ran after them. Once or twice they thought they were called over to their clearing but they had always fled. But after the Poes incident nobody went spying again, so whether they were still there or not, nobody knew for sure.

Pombreol, on the other hand, was willing to take the risk of leaving those strange men alone in the forest,

Pombreol

for he couldn't imagine how he would take his two wives and his three young children away. Most of all, he wanted to know if there was any truth in the teaching that was handed down from generation to generation that went like this: *'If the man with no toes and body but fingers and head only arrives in this land, things will never be the same again'*. Pombreol for one didn't want the same for his family. He had enough deaths already. If this was the dawning of a new day so be it....

Eighteen

THE OLD HAS GONE & THE NEW HAS COME

After a few days Pombreol and a few others from his tribe did go and see the strangers in their forest but they had disappeared again. They wondered when and where they went. A few suggested that, as the strangers were staying within the tribesmen's sacrificial grounds, the gods may have gotten angry and eaten them. They could simply be the spirits of our ancestors, someone else mentioned. Still others suggested that they had disappeared to get more re-enforcements.

Whatever the reason for their disappearance, it didn't matter, as long as there was peace in their area. At least men were able to rest peacefully without having to worry about the strangers in their territory.

A few days had passed and to Pombreol's uttermost surprise, the strangers did come back again. This time, not to the forest but right to their village. Two white men, two brown and one very black man made up the team this time.

Pombreol

The men of the village stood their grounds. They had been running away from these strangers for the past number of days and Pombreol wasn't sure if he wanted to run or hide again. This time, he stood his ground and looked at the strangers fearfully.

All the women and children fled in all directions but Pombreol and his men stayed close together at one corner of their ceremonial ground, not daring to run away like the women and children. As far as Pombreol was concerned, these were not the men in the forest. They were another group. The strangers in sign languages told them to get closer to them.

At first they hesitated but, seeing that there was no sign of danger they walked slowly towards them, watching suspiciously and ready to run at any time if something did happen. As they walked closer, one of the white men put his hands into those funny clothes he was wearing and brought out a small bundle. Using his one hand he poured some white stuff on his hands and started to lick his fingers. He then pointed at one of the men standing nearby and asked him to open his hands.

The man immediately opened his fisted hand, onto which some of the white stuff was poured by the strangers. Following the strangers lead, he tasted the stuff, which looked like white ashes in his open hand. To their disbelieve, the man was licking his hands now.

The rest of the men followed the first one, wanting to taste this thing. Each man reached out with a open palm and a bit of the white stuff was poured on their hands. They all tasted it and it tasted like their traditional salt, except that this one was tastier. The visitors gave them a few more strange things and went off, leaving Pombreol and his men wondering where they came from and where they were going.

Pombreol

Pombreol and his men stood there staring at each other when the women and children came out of their hiding place and the men explained to them what had just happened. They discussed it for a while and walked slowly home, still hanging their heads in disbelief.

Pombreol gathered his family and told them that these strangers had a special odour about them. He carefully explained to his anxious family that when the strangers are close they could smell a distinctive smell. He wondered what the white men rub on their body to smell like this. Sanowi wanted to know if the smell was nauseating. Pombreol tried to explain but he couldn't find the right words so he told them, he did not feel like vomiting but he was not sure if he liked it either. One thing he was sure of, finding out the source of their body smell was going to be his first assignment when they came back.

The next day Pombreol and his family were hard at work in the garden when Sanowi, who was resting nearby, ran to her parents and told them she could smell something strange. Pombreol stopped immediately and took a deep breath. Suddenly he dropped his digging stick and told his family to hide because the strangers were nearby.

As he stood on the lookout, the strangers did come. This time there was many of them. He stood quietly where he was. For some reason these people always made him feel very small and uncomfortable. He gathered what little courage he had and stared at them suspiciously. As they approached him, the smell of their body overpowered him and he sat down. They smiled and said something to him but he did not understand.

Then they gave him more of the white stuff, the same that had his whole family producing more saliva when they had tasted the first lot on the previous day. Then, after talking to him in some sign language, they walked past him. He was speechless as he watched them go on their way. He wasn't sure if he really understood what they were saying in their sign language and was still wondering about it when his family gathered around him and started asking him questions. He simply gathered his gardening tools and walked home. Without looking back, he told his family to follow him. His family were surprised at his sudden change of mood and followed him quickly to the village.

Back in the village, all the people were gathered in the ceremonial grounds and the talk was all about the strangers with the strange smell.

"Surely, they do not look like spirit-men, they look strong, and they are talking and eating as well and so I am very confused," the chief concluded.

"Even their body smell is nothing like the smell of a dead man," Pombreol added.

"Their body smell is almost like the smell of the presence of a cuscus during moonlight hunting," someone else pointed out and a few nodded their heads in agreement.

The more the talk about the stranger's strange smell, the more urgency Pombreol felt to find out what the strangers rub on their body so it produces such a smell that you immediately feel their presence without seeing them. Whatever it takes, he would find out this time.

A few days later the strangers arrived again. This time they made signs for all the men of the village to follow them. In the next clan's ceremonial ground all the men from various clans had gathered. After several exchanges in sign language, all the men understood that they were to help the strangers to cut the trees down and make a road to where the strangers were coming from. In exchange for their work, they will be given articles such as tiny coloured glass beads, more of the white stuff, very sharp smaller knives and some more very strange things as well.

Pombreol was asked to look into one of those strange articles. As he walked up and looked into this small article that one of the strangers was holding, he almost choked himself when someone looking exactly like himself stared back at him! When he regained his strength, he ran all the way home. Nobody dared to stop him as they saw the fear in his eyes.

At home Pombreol's voice trailed off as he recalled the experiences of the day. Why was he looking back at himself when he was looking into that shiny article? Do those strangers perform magic? Is that how they separated his spirit from himself? Was that his spirit staring back at him? Did they put his spirit back into himself when he ran away? How about the other men of the clan? Did they also experience the same thing? And why did they want a big and wide track to reach where they were coming from? Did they have people as big and wide as the roads they said to help them build? He would find out later when they were back but right now his head was aching in total confusion, so he just laid down flat on the grass on the ceremonial ground.

The men arrived in the evening and told Pombreol that he was the first and last person to have looked into that shiny article. After he ran away, the shiny thing was hidden in fear that every man will run away like him. He paused for a moment or two and then announced abruptly, "I am going back to those strangers tomorrow and find out the truth behind all these things."

Pombreol

In the days that followed all the men were busy felling trees, cutting grass and digging the earth towards the southern side. They were making a bigger pathway for people to walk to the place where these strangers were coming from. As they worked, Pombreol tried his best to work close to one of those white men so he could observe them closely. A crowd of strange brown men were there but he had no eyes for them.

They seemed to be very tall, big and white. Pombreol watched them and listened to their talk, all the time wondering about what they were saying, where they came from and the strange food they were eating.

When he mentioned that to his clansmen, one of them said he saw the white man going out to the bush to defecate. So they decided to examine his waste to see if the colour was yellow, red or white like he was. They quietly walked up to the waste site, got a stick and examined it. In disbelief they were all staring at a waste product actually like their own. They walked slowly back to their own village pondering this information.

Each day they were given goods as payment for their labour. They were either given coloured tiny beads which were used for body decorations, tasty white stuff or a small sharp knife. People got very excited and the numbers of workers grew when they heard about the shiny steel axes and the strange food they cooked and gave them to eat.

The strange foods were served on their flat banana leaves and the men would tie them with bush vines and take them to their family, who were slowly getting used to the taste and really looking forward to that meal of *elicesh* (rice). Bags of sweet potatoes, greens, bananas and other native foods were given to those white men in exchange for their one cooked meal. The people of the land were willing to give them those things as their strange foods were so tasty and they wanted more of those foods.

In the hectic activity of those days Pombreol forgot his mission for joining the white men until, one day, he was asked to accompany a few of the strange men to his father's side of the lands over the mountains. As they climbed up the mountains and down into the valley, walking through narrow, rough and muddy native tracks, everybody felt exhausted and stopped over a water fall.

As Pombreol watched, the strangers removed their clothes and jumped into the pool created by the waterfall. He was afraid they were going to get drunk and told them so, but they didn't seem to understand. As he continued to stare fearfully at them, they got a piece of something out of their bag and started to rub it hard into their wet bodies. It looked like a piece of pig's fat only it was hard like a flat stone.

Strangely, it produced some kind of bubbles on their body. He moved closer to watch yet another strange happening unfolding before his eyes, when the smell hit him. The smell was so strong he sat down in dizziness. Then the realisation hit him hard and he wanted to run back and tell his family and his clansmen about the discovery. Now he knew the cause of the smell in the stranger's presence. It was this thing they were using to rub on their wet bodies.

In his excitement he told the strangers about his discovery, but nobody seemed to understand him. Instead they were calling to him and making sign language gestures for him to jump into the pool. He had never ever in his whole life jumped into the water and he

Pombreol

wondered what they were up to. In the midst of all their sign language they seemed to be repeating one word, and that word seemed to be "wash, wash".

Pombreol did not know what was going on until all of a sudden he was in the pool with the strangers! One of them had pulled him into the river and they were splashing water on him. The next minute they were rubbing the smelly stuff on his hair and the rest of his body. He tried to open his eyes but the thing being rubbed on his body was causing a stinging in his eyes so he was unable to open them. They all seemed to be brushing his whole body too. After what seemed to be a very long time, they rinsed him off and released him.

When he came out of the pool, he felt totally brand new and fresh. He didn't look so black anymore as all his accumulated dirt was washed away. He felt almost like one of the strangers - and smelt just like them too!

When he was again offered that glassy equipment to peep in, he was so lightheaded after the pool experience that he accepted it and looked bravely into the glass. This time a brand new Pombreol was staring back at him. He opened his mouth wide, and this action was also happening inside the glass. He performed all kinds of facial expressions and the image of himself inside the glass was imitating all that he was doing. He now understood that they used this equipment to look at themselves as they were presently.

He quickly got some fresh tanget leaves to cover his now clean bottom, and walked back home whistling brightly. He had now found out, just as he had promised his family he would, the story behind the smelling presence of the strangers and the shiny glass that shows someone like themselves staring right back at them.

Pombreol

Now he was on his way home to show them.

The old Pombreol with all the dirt of the past was gone, behold, he was a new man with a new image. And he was ready to face the future of the new era……..

About the Author

Stella Sondpi grew up in the Mendi area of the Southern Highlands of Papua New Guinea, listening to the stories told by Pombreol, her grandfather. After secondary education she completed nursing training, working then in various capacities as a nurse in several provinces. She now works as Deputy Director of Nursing at Mendi Hospital. This is her first book.

Pombreol with his last wife and a grandchild after outside world contact.
Photo taken in 1992

www.ingramcontent.com/pod-product-compliance
Lightning Source LLC
Chambersburg PA
CBHW050312010526
44107CB00055B/2214